The

ARTIST'S WAY

for

PARENTS

Also by Julia Cameron

Jeremy P. Tarcher/Penguin
a member of Penguin Group (USA)
New York

The

ARTIST'S WAY

for

PARENTS

RAISING CREATIVE CHILDREN

JULIA CAMERON

with Emma Lively

JEREMY P. TARCHER/PENGUIN
Published by the Penguin Group
Penguin Group (USA), 375 Hudson Street,
New York, New York 10014, USA

USA · Canada · UK · Ireland · Australia
New Zealand · India · South Africa · China

Penguin Books Ltd, Registered Offices: 80 Strand, London WC2R 0RL, England
For more information about the Penguin Group visit penguin.com

Most Tarcher/Penguin books are available at special quantity discounts for bulk purchase
for sales promotions, premiums, fund-raising, and educational needs. Special books or book
excerpts also can be created to fit specific needs. For details, write Penguin Group (USA)
Special Markets, 375 Hudson Street, New York, NY 10014.

Library of Congress Cataloging-in-Publication Data

Cameron, Julia.
The artist's way for parents: raising creative children / Julia Cameron with Emma Lively.
p.   cm.
Includes index.
ISBN 978-0-399-16372-2
1. Creative ability in children.   2. Child rearing.   I. Lively, Emma.   II. Title.
BF723.C7C36   2013   2013009654
155.4'1335—dc23

Printed in the United States of America
1   3   5   7   9   10   8   6   4   2

Book design by Meighan Cavanaugh

Some names and identifying characteristics have been
changed to protect the piracy of the individuals involved.

While the authors have made every effort to provide accurate telephone numbers,
Internet addresses, and other contact information at the time of publication, neither the
publisher nor the authors assume any responsibility for errors, or for changes that occur
after publication. Further, the publisher does not have any control over and does
not assume any responsibility for author or third-party websites or their content.

The Artist's Way for Parents

is dedicated to

Dorothy and James Cameron

and

Martha and Robert Lively,

who raised creative children.

Parenting is a great adventure. Awakening your child's sense of curiosity and wonder helps you reawaken your own. Reawakening your own sense of curiosity and wonder helps you awaken your child's.

—JULIA CAMERON

Contents

Foreword

Looking up from my Morning Pages into my daughter Serafina's eyes, I am amazed. She gleefully discovered peekaboo today, grabbing the wet cloth I was using to wipe away the orange smears of squash on her face. Grinning wildly, she shrieked, fixing me with her giant baby-blue eyes, pausing to see what I would do next. "There you are!" I cheered. Again, she held the cloth over her face and then, bursting into peals of laughter, she peeked out proud and happy. I loved it—scrawling the scene into my journal that has become a glorious chronicle of Serafina's many "firsts."

To see her eyes sparkle as she plays is pure delight. They speak volumes, often quite serious, unwavering, brewing—"giving me the business" I call it. These are the moments when I think of my mother, Julia. My mother can deliver that same look, announcing, "I am a mother who would!" The words and the glare full of all the promise and threat implied. Fierce, formidable, and very creative—being on the receiving end of "the business" is not for the faint of heart. This daring streak, combined with my mother's tenacity and ingenuity, has made her one of my greatest teachers and champions.

This very book is a prime example—a gift—for me and others who are looking to nurture our children and ourselves. In my better moments as a new mom, finding my way through Serafina's first year, I am discovering who my daughter is and learning who I am as her mother. I am discovering the space between the idea of "the mother I should be" and the mother I actually am—the mother whom Serafina needs me to be. Then there are those moments I find myself wondering and worrying, as I am apt to do. "Am I a good mom?" "Is this enough?" "Am I enough?" And, "Am I doing it right enough?"

Again, I think of my mom. Twenty-five years ago, she asked me if I thought she was a "good mom." At eleven years old, I piped up, "You are a FUN mom!" I did not see "good" and "fun" as mutually exclusive. A serious child, I needed fun. My mother recognized I needed our adventures—roller-skating around the apartment, driving cross-country, or jumping horses. I needed the opportunity she gave me to be a kid, bravely exploring and enjoying life. Now, I see how so many of my mother's choices were based on what I needed. She did her utmost to provide opportunities for me to grow into who I am—not just "grow up."

When my mother taught me to jump horses, I remember her instructing me to look up over the fence and she would call out, "Now! Throw your heart over the jump!" Sure enough, my Shetland pony, Silver Lilly, would spring up over the little cross rail and we were flying! This is one of the many ways my mother taught me how to practice faith in action. My mother encouraged me to see how far I could go. I'm grateful to her for infusing my life with a sense of creative adventure. I hope to do the same for my daughter. I don't know if Serafina will like horses, but I'm looking forward to finding out.

In the meantime, our adventures are more tame: "mini Artist Dates," rocking out in the produce aisle with exotic fruits and vegetables or strolling through the greenhouse at the Botanic Gardens to see orchids and bougainvillea in the middle of a Midwest winter. I seek signs of spring on our very bundled-up walks; pointing out the red-breasted robins, the daffodils and crocuses popping up amidst the manicured planters of pansies. This is Serafina's first spring; sharing it with her, I see the world anew while taking comfort in the perennial cycles.

—*Domenica Cameron-Scorsese*

INTRODUCTION

～

Twenty years ago, I published a book called *The Artist's Way*. Its premise, that creativity is a spiritual matter and that we are all creative, struck a chord with the reading audience. Nearly four million people bought *The Artist's Way* and worked with its toolkit. When I would go out to teach, people would approach me with gifts.

"I used your tools and this is what I made," they would say, handing me a book, a CD, or a DVD. But with the gifts often came a request: "I'm a parent. Could you write a book about creativity in children?"

"No," I always laughed. "If you want your children to be creative, practice creativity yourself. Children learn from what we do." I would face down the disappointment in my petitioners. I truly believed that if they worked their Artist's Way program, they would come upon imaginative and innovative ways to parent.

But perhaps my answer was too thin. Year after year, request after request, I resisted because I thought that children were *already* creative, and that their parents could always use the basic Artist's Way text to free themselves creatively and set an example for their children. But what of the parents who were not already familiar with *The Artist's Way*? The early years of parenting were an unlikely time for busy parents to launch into an intensive creative recovery of their own. What assumptions was I making about creative parenting based on my own immersion in a creative life? What assumptions was I making based on my own parents' parenting—which had been colorful and encouraging? Perhaps there were lessons that could—and should—be taught.

For two decades, people have asked me to write this book.

And so, why now? As my own daughter embarks upon her new journey as a wife and mother, I find myself rethinking my position, wanting to give my daughter a practical toolkit that she can use in her mothering. I want to pass on the tools I myself used as well as the tools my own very creative mother employed.

I come from a family of seven children. Every single one of us makes our living by our wits. My older sister, Connie, is a writer, my brother, Jaimie, is a musician, my sister, Libby, is a painter, my brother, Christopher, is a musician, and my sister, Lorrie, is another writer, as is my youngest sister, Pegi.

As for my mother, she was a poet who loved mothering. She kept a large bulletin board where she posted our latest artwork. Each holiday was marked by thematically related art projects. We made ghosts and goblins for Halloween, we made snowflakes for

Christmas, we made Valentine's Day cards, and we made Easter eggs. All of us worked on our projects at the big oak dining room table. Boys and girls alike tried their hand at crafts. Our mother displayed our efforts along the wall of our spiral staircase. She taught us the art of making snowflake cutouts, and our flakes were posted on every available window.

Between holidays, our mother still made sure we had art supplies. I remember drawing a rearing palomino horse, which my father framed and hung in the family room. There was no sense of competition among the siblings. We were encouraged to delight in one another's gifts. In this regard, our parents set a good example, always thrilled by what we had wrought.

Somehow, my parents never conveyed to us the message of our culture: that it was difficult to make money as an artist, or that being an artist wasn't a "real" job. Exercising our creativity was always regarded as a worthwhile endeavor. When we told them of our dreams, they never said, "Oh, sweetheart, don't you think you need something to fall back on?" Instead, they supported our belief that we could do—and even make a living doing—what we loved.

Looking back, I see my parents as unusual, even radical, in their stubborn support of our creativity. Regardless of cultural norms, they unapologetically placed deep value on creating a culture of healthy creativity in the home. Is it a coincidence—or any wonder—that we all grew up to make our living using our creative gifts? Did this upbringing set the stage for the concepts I would articulate and develop in *The Artist's Way* and in thirty more books beyond it?

I'm not a parenting expert. I'm a creativity expert. I am a parent, however, and I used creativity tools in mothering my own child. As she grew up, she reflected back to me my belief that there are few things more inherent—or precious—in children than their creativity. Creativity is a spiritual undertaking. Parenting is also a spiritual undertaking. We are entrusted with the care of our children's souls as well as their bodies. There are—and will always be—myriad books on the science of child development. *The Artist's Way for Parents* is not one of them. It is a spiritual toolkit, a support, a guide.

In a culture of "more," the "more" applies to parenting as well. We are perfectionists and we want our children to be perfect. We obsess about the outcome of our actions as we hover above our children, trying to provide every opportunity, every bit of knowledge and exposure. We worry about our toddler's college education. We think, as parents, that we must be very serious. But we are serious enough. It is a healthy dose of joy that our children require. Let us loosen our grip on the obsession with perfection, with the "mastery" of parenting, and allow ourselves to explore and delight in the mystery instead.

And so, a toolkit: For children, healthy guidance and encouragement of their creative gifts. For parents, companionship, structure, support. Every child—and every parent—is creative. For some of us, it may be easier to see our children's creativity than our own. As we take in their openness and sense of possibility, we may find that they remind us of our own potential, as well. Exercising our creativity is an act of faith, which connects us to a higher power. When we are willing to explore our creative gifts, we allow both ourselves and our children to connect to something greater—and to each other.

I will use the word "God" in this book. Please do not let semantics stop you from experimenting with the concepts within. No matter what you call it—the source, the force, the universe, the Tao—there is a benevolent Something greater than ourselves to which we can connect. We can find a spiritual path regardless of our religious upbringing, which, for many of us, may have lapsed. Fostering our children's creativity, we are fostering our children's spirituality as well. Parents and children have independent and direct relationships to a higher power, and so both always have an unlimited supply of spiritual support available to them. This book will help parents and children alike tap into that source.

Every child has different needs at different times. And yet the same spiritual tools provide answers over and over. This sourcebook focuses on universal concepts that parents can return to again and again as their children evolve. It functions as a gentle reminder that we are all spiritual beings with creativity stamped into our DNA. The smallest bit of spiritual encouragement yields large results. Divided into twelve chapters, each with a spiritual theme and accompanying exercises, *The Artist's Way for Parents* is aimed at parents with children newborn through age twelve. It is never too early—or too late—to nurture children's creativity. Working with this book, parents replenish their own creative stores as well as nurture those of their children, giving them valuable tools for the journey toward adulthood.

Parenting is a great adventure. The early years of parenting can be one of the most inspiring chapters of your life, opening you to love and growth you may not have yet experienced. Using these years to tap into your own creativity as well as your child's, you will love and grow together. Awakening your child's sense of curiosity and wonder helps you reawaken your own. Reawakening your own sense of curiosity and wonder helps you awaken your child's. Exercising creativity, alone and together, strengthens the bond between parent and child. Funded by optimism, your child is guided to an expansive and adventurous life.

THE THREE BASIC TOOLS

The Artist's Way for Parents utilizes three basic tools: Morning Pages, Creative Expeditions, and Highlights. These tools, when used in conjunction with one another, will help you to develop a sense of guidance, energy, and clarity as you explore the many healthy creative impulses that will arise for you and for your children. Used consistently, these tools will give you a spiritual foundation and an ongoing sense of structure and safety.

1. Morning Pages—three pages of longhand daily writing that the parent does alone

The bedrock tool of a creative recovery—or discovery—is something I call Morning Pages. Done first thing, they siphon off negativity as they provoke, clarify, comfort, cajole, prioritize, and synchronize the day at hand. Sometimes parents feel that they have lost their right to privacy, but this does not have to be the case. Morning Pages are for your eyes only. They are a safe place to vent, muse, strategize, and dream. There is no wrong way to do

Morning Pages. Just write longhand—yes, longhand—for three pages, about anything, and then stop. Do not share your Morning Pages with anyone. I have had students shred, burn, hide, or lock up their Morning Pages. I myself have often joked that in my will, it should state, "First, cremate the Morning Pages. Then take care of the body." Morning Pages are a portable, private support kit for the parent. Parenting is an emotional experience, and you are allowed to have all of the feelings you are experiencing. Morning Pages are a safe place for you to process these feelings, ultimately making you able to be more present in your day—and with your child.

"But Julia!" my students sometimes exclaim. "I don't have time to get up and do Morning Pages before my child wakes up." I tell them to do as many Pages as they can before their child wakes, and then to go about their family duties, finishing the Pages as they can. In a perfect world, we would all have time to get Morning Pages done in their entirety. But it is better to get them done piecemeal than not at all. What is important here is that you have a place to safely process turbulent emotions. Virginia Woolf said that a writer needed "a room of her own," by which I take it that she meant all writers need privacy and solitude. I would extend this advice to include everybody, not just writers, and most especially parents. Viewed this way, the Morning Pages can be seen as a private, portable "room of your own." At first, it may be tempting to share them, but within weeks of having started the process, the importance of their privacy will be revealed.

I invented Morning Pages when my daughter was a toddler and I was feeling overwhelmed by her demands for my attention.

I began getting up earlier than my daughter and taking myself quickly to the page. I was having a feeling common to many new mothers: *I don't know who I am anymore.* The Pages helped me make contact with myself.

Morning Pages are not intended to be "art." Rather, they are "artless." The simple act of moving the hand across the page puts us into contact with our authentic self. It is important that they are written longhand. Most of us are able to go faster by computer. But faster is not better. In this case, velocity is the enemy.

Picture yourself driving a car, speeding along at seventy-five miles an hour. "Oops! Was that my exit? Was that a gas station or a convenience store?" This is what it is like to write Morning Pages on the computer.

Now picture yourself driving more temperately, at fifty-five: "Here comes a gas station," and "It's my exit—there's a convenience store, too." In other words, Morning Pages allow you to place yourself precisely in the landscape of your life.

I often think of Morning Pages as a form of meditation uniquely suited to hyperactive Westerners. It is very difficult for most of us to sit for twenty minutes and do nothing. Pages allow you to sit and do *something*. With Pages we are saying, "This is what I like, this is what I don't like. . . . This is what I want more of, this is what I want less of." It is as if we are sending a telegram to the Universe.

"But Julia! I'm already shy on sleep," I can hear you protesting. I need to tell you that I sympathize, and promise you that the Morning Pages will bring you time and energy.

When I began writing Morning Pages, I was a single mother. Domenica and I were living in Taos, New Mexico, in an adobe house at the end of a winding dirt road. The house had windows looking north to Taos Mountain. I would get up early and take myself to a long pine table where I faced north. I don't know where the idea came from for me to write three pages daily, but that is what I did, rising as the sun cleared the mountains. At first my Pages were grumpy and griping. I was asking them what direction I should take next. At the time, I was a Hollywood screenwriter, and my scripts kept being bought but not made. I was discouraged. And then, one morning as I was finishing my Morning Pages, a character strolled into my consciousness along with the idea, "You could write a novel, not a movie." And so I did. Every day I would write my Morning Pages and then turn my hand to writing a novel. The Pages had seen my creative dilemma and offered me a solution. As time went on, I found my Pages offering me solutions for problems of many stripes. Finishing my novel, my Pages made it clear to me that I didn't really want to live down a dirt road in an adobe house. Maybe someday, just not now. Instead, the Pages suggested I should go back to New York. When I did that, I received the marching orders that told me I was to teach.

I remember it all so clearly: I was walking in Greenwich Village, and I was praying for another writing idea. What I heard clearly was the directive, "Teach." I was horrified. I didn't want to teach. I thought that teaching would squelch my own inner artist. Heading home from my walk, I called a girlfriend.

"Regina," I said. "I've been called to teach."

"Ahh," said Regina. "I'll call you right back."

True to her word, she phoned me fifteen minutes later.

"Congratulations," she said. "You're now on the faculty of the New York Feminist Art Institute, and your first class gathers on Thursday."

And so it was that I started teaching, assigning my students three pages of morning writing and discovering, for them as for me, that the Pages led to breakthroughs.

I noticed that this phenomenon seemed particularly true for parents. Although they protested that they "couldn't" do them, they in fact did do them, and excitedly reported insights and ideas that came tumbling onto the page. The loneliness of parenting made the Pages an all-the-more-valuable companion. At last, someone to talk to.

I urge you to try Morning Pages, and discover the results for yourself.

2. CREATIVE EXPEDITION—A ONCE-WEEKLY DUAL ADVENTURE THAT THE PARENT AND CHILD PLAN, LOOK FORWARD TO, AND TAKE TOGETHER

A Creative Expedition doesn't need to be large, but it does need to be festive. The point is to refill our spiritual coffers. When looking for ideas for Creative Expeditions, think whimsy, frivolity, fun. Depending on the age of your children, they may be actively involved in choosing the destination.

Natasha, a stay-at-home mom, started taking Creative Expeditions when her child was still an infant. "I knew I needed to get out of the house. The fresh air was good for me and for my daughter. I would put her in her carrier and venture out to a place that I would enjoy. Sometimes it was a museum, sometimes it was a shoe store. I could tell that even though my child was too young to experience the places herself, she was alert and taking in the images. I could tell the change of scenery interested her and made her happy, as it did me. As my daughter got older, she helped me choose the adventures. I took her to zoos and toy stores, aquariums and concerts. Even though I might have done this anyway, the act of making a point of it, planning the outing and looking forward to it, made all the difference. It forced me to come up with a new adventure every week. It's been one of the favorite things my daughter and I do together."

For parents of older or multiple children, the act of organizing Creative Expeditions can bring a sense of magic into the home. Minette, a mother of four, rotates which son gets to choose the adventure of the week.

"My oldest, Cormic, is twelve and loves planning the Creative Expedition," Minette says. "He's very protective of his three younger brothers, and he takes pride in choosing something that everyone will enjoy. I feel like he's getting some good experience with parenting, really. Having multiple children is a balancing act. But there are adventures that everyone can participate in. It is always a bonding experience for our family. The older my kids get, the more responsibility they take—and the more interested they are in taking responsibility in the first place."

For parent and child, the commitment to planned "fun" can be a highlight of the week—and one of the most important parts of developing consistency and wonder in the lives of our children. It is important that Creative Expeditions do not evolve into shopping trips. A visit to the zoo or an aquarium is preferable to visiting a toy store.

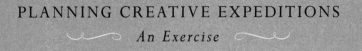

PLANNING CREATIVE EXPEDITIONS
An Exercise

List five Creative Expeditions that you could take with your child, such as visits to the zoo, a children's museum, a new playground, a cathedral, and the library.

1. _____

2. _____

3. _____

4. _____

5. _____

3. HIGHLIGHTS—A DAILY BEDTIME RITUAL IN WHICH THE PARENT AND CHILD EACH SHARE THEIR FAVORITE MOMENT FROM THE DAY

Many mothers and fathers reach day's end tired—and even crabby. Tucking their child into bed, they are ready for the day to be over. But bedtime can be a time of restorative ritual. The third tool, Highlights, helps to end the day on a positive note. "Here was my very favorite part of the day," the parent says. "It was when we went to the dog park and watched the dogs play. What was your favorite part of the day?"

"I liked swinging," their child may reply, or even, "Me, too," also picking the dog park.

"Yes. It was fun to push you on the swing," or "Yes—I thought you were enjoying those puppies." The habit of looking for the positive is something that makes each day's march into a game.

Domenica and I practiced this nightly ritual. Now, living in separate cities, we still maintain the routine of a daily check-in. Our conversations need not be long for us to connect and feel up to date with each other's lives as we quickly review the most memorable parts of our day.

A habit of reviewing the day's highlights is a habit of forging happy memories.

Chapter One

CULTIVATING SAFETY

Every child is an artist. The problem is how to remain an artist once he grows up.

—PABLO PICASSO

reativity is born in generosity, and flourishes where there is a sense of safety and acceptance. For our children to thrive, we must cultivate this safe environment. To do this, we must be willing to take steps toward our own creative and spiritual health as well. Taking care of ourselves, we give ourselves the energy and clarity to take care of our children. Like the advice we receive on an airplane to administer our own air masks before helping the children beside us, we must nurture ourselves to set the example for our children. Because a happy, creative home grows from a happy, creative parent, we must begin by focusing on finding creative approaches to the common and challenging realities of the parenting role. With a few simple tools, we

can embrace this journey with a light touch and an open heart, establishing a lively and contagious sense of spiritual safety in our home.

SETTING THE STAGE

Children mimic what we do—playing with trucks or taking care of dolls, they imitate adult behaviors from a very young age. They also absorb and reflect our attitudes and emotional states. When we're stressed, they pick up on it. When we're joyful, they mirror our delight. When we feel safe, our children feel safe. When we model genuine enthusiasm, our children learn to have passions. It is one of the great joys of parenting to notice the ways in which our children learn from our example. We, as parents, provide the example for how a life is lived.

Desi, mother to six-year-old Aaron, works as a nurse, and her husband, Eric, has a career as a firefighter. Aaron has a collection of toy fire trucks—gifts from his dad—that he counts among his most prized possessions. "He is absolutely sure that he's responding to emergencies when he plays with those trucks," Desi laughs. "He says he's a hero, like Daddy. He's right." Aaron's connection to his toy fire trucks is actually a connection to his dad.

When Domenica was in kindergarten, I walked her to and from school daily. Although I varied the route, our favorite way to go involved passing a fish store. Taking Domenica by the hand, I led her into the dark interior. I pointed her toward the tank where a matched pair of angelfish floated. "Pretty, but mean," I told her. Next, I led her to the tank containing a flotilla of swordtails. As we approached, the fish made a mad dash to hide behind a coral formation. "Pretty, but shy," I told my daughter.

"Mommy, look!" she piped up, leading the way to a tank full of fantailed goldfish. As we approached, they swam closer, as interested in us as we were in them. "Pretty, but not shy," I explained, making a mental note to myself that Domenica was old enough to enjoy a fish tank. For her sixth birthday, I gave her a pair of fantailed goldfish in a tank the size of a small TV. She was delighted with the present. Years later, when Domenica went away to college, she got a fish tank for her dorm room. "It makes it feel like home," she explained. I smiled to myself, remembering our walks to school and marveling at how that simple stop had made an impact.

As much as we must make a conscious effort to reach out to our children, we must also make a conscious effort to "reach out" to ourselves, paying attention to our own needs and desires.

As parents, we often make the mistake of thinking we need to be completely available to our children at all times—anything less would be "bad parenting." But what exactly are we role-modeling for our children if we abandon ourselves in the name of generosity? Becoming a parent is an act of selflessness indeed—but we must still maintain our sense of self if we are to have anything to give to our children.

When my daughter was a toddler, I was a single mother. I had the job of supporting us with my writing. I couldn't afford not to write, and so I became a writer with child. I taught myself how to write with my daughter crawling underfoot. "Mommy's writing," I would say, as I set her to play with her toy horses. I learned to dash my thoughts to the page, writing quickly.

"Mommy," my daughter would interrupt.

"Mommy's working," I would reiterate. "Mommy's writing."

Soon my daughter learned that I would give her my attention once I was finished with the page. She began to interrupt me less and to turn her own focus to her playthings. Soon she realized "I'm playing" to be a boundary, just like "I'm writing." She modeled the concentration that she saw me display. With a little jolt, I realized I was teaching my daughter valuable autonomy. As I dipped into my imagination to write, she dipped into her imagination to play. When I finished my sprint to the page, my daughter would then claim my focus.

"Which horse is your favorite?" I would ask her. She liked the golden palomino. "That's my favorite, too," I told her. And together we would place the little statuette in a shoebox that served as a stall.

"How do you find time to write?" my friends would sometimes ask me. I told them of Domenica's toy horses, and the boundary I set: "Mommy's writing."

"But doesn't Domenica resent it?" asked another mother, who set no boundaries, being always "on call" for her child. As time passed, I noticed that her child was becoming a little greedy for her mother's constant attention. I remember a play date when I got out the toy horses and set the two children to play. Soon our little visitor wanted my attention. That was when I heard Domenica say, "Mommy's writing." No, Domenica did not resent my writing. In fact, before long, she began to write herself. As the years passed, the toy horses gave way to journals. She wrote poetry, short stories, brief plays—the very things I had been writing as she played with her golden palomino at my feet.

SETTING THE STAGE FOR ENTHUSIASM
An Exercise

List five things you love, such as snow, cherry pie, parrots, gerbera daisies, and drumming.

1. _____
   _____
2. _____
   _____
3. _____
   _____
4. _____
   _____
5. _____
   _____

How could you share each of these things with your child? For example:

Snow—Cut out snowflakes.
Cherry pie—Bake Grandma's recipe.
Parrots—Visit a bird store.
Gerbera daisies—Go to the plant store together and buy one gerbera daisy, then come home and draw the flower together.
Drumming—Make a drum from an oatmeal container.

Now choose one item from your list, and embark on exploring it with your child.

ISOLATION

Becoming a parent requires us to both add things to—and remove things from—our lives as we knew them. Added to our lives are a crib and changing table, and removed are spontaneous evenings out and a sleep schedule dictated by our own level of fatigue. Feeling isolated can be a natural part of this transition and is by no means a failing on your part. It is important, however, to make a habit of not isolating yourself. As powerless as we may feel over the great swaths of time alone with our child, we are not actually powerless. Using a few simple strategies, it is possible to protect ourselves from the pain of isolation—and this is important both for our well-being and our children's.

Isolation as a parent takes two forms: one is being alienated from friends, and the other is being alienated from yourself. When you are able to stay in touch with the many different parts of yourself, then you will be better able to navigate the changing relationships—and time alone—that you will encounter as a parent.

Yesterday my phone rang. It was a new mother on the other end of the line.

"I just need to hear another adult," my caller explained.

"Motherhood getting to you?" I asked.

"I'm afraid so," she laughed. "My son is good company, but not all the company I need." My caller was right about that. Like many other mothers, she found herself suffering the pangs of isolation. She also found herself suffering from guilt. "I should be more fulfilled," she reasoned. But even as she focused her time and attention on her child, she found herself still yearning for adult conversation. What she didn't know was that her yearnings and sense of guilt about those yearnings were normal. I couldn't offer to come across the country and babysit for an hour, but I could listen to her for the few free minutes she had. I could understand and relate to her, and mirror her feelings back as the same ones I had experienced as a new parent. I could remind her that she wasn't alone.

Before my daughter's birth, I made my living as a movie journalist. I would go away on location with a film and spend long days on set, surrounded by the crew. I enjoyed this work, and I loved being able to ask pointed questions of each crew member. They were all too happy to talk about their jobs, convinced, correctly, that the film could not be made without them. This was true for lighting, sound, costumes—the many and varied categories of film expertise. When I became pregnant with Domenica, I found myself feeling out of place. My filmmaker's uniform—blue jeans and a T-shirt—gave way to maternity clothes. Although crew members were chivalrous, I found myself feeling left out. I fought these feelings, but they were there.

I had Domenica on Labor Day, our only day off in the twenty-two-week schedule. When the car came to drive me home, daughter in arms, I instructed the driver to take us not home, but to the sound stage at MGM where Domenica's father was shooting. I showed the baby off proudly—she was a beautiful infant. But soon it was time for my husband and his crew to turn their attention back to filmmaking, and it was my job to take the baby home. I found myself feeling isolated and afraid, even as Domenica slept soundly in the crib I had carefully prepared for her. My days were now my daughter's days. When my husband came home, I was eager to hear of life on the set, and I was keenly aware that my stories of our daughter's day were repetitive. She ate, she slept, she played, and I was her captive audience. My husband loved our daughter, but he was not spellbound by her antics. As for me, I had lost my role as his playmate. Increasingly, I was "Mommy," and I missed my former self. When our daughter was less than a year old, my marriage disintegrated. With typewriter and child, I moved into a house of my own.

Now I was really isolated. My days consisted of childcare and work. I wrote whenever Domenica was napping or absorbed in her playpen with her toys. Wanting to be a good mother, I made the mistake of thinking motherhood was a job that left no room for me. It was a 24/7 job, I told myself. Without a co-parent, this child depended on me and me alone. I had no choice, no other option. Ideas I might have that didn't involve my daughter would just have to wait, be put off, or forgotten altogether. Increasingly, I became irritable and discontented. I felt tethered on a short leash. It was then that my friend Julianna McCarthy, older and wiser, instructed me to hire a babysitter and get out of the house on my own. "You need to nurture yourself first," she advised me.

Taking her at her word, I hired a sitter and took my first "break" from motherhood. "You'll see how much better you feel when you put yourself first," Julie counseled me. I did feel better. I had more patience, more whimsy, more optimism. I was more available to Domenica's feelings, humor, and ideas—as well as my own. And so, a habit of once-a-week solo expeditions, the forerunner of Artist Dates, was established.

It is important not to let ourselves become housebound. Isolation leads to depression and feelings of being trapped. Home alone with our child, we may feel disconnected and depressed. And having those feelings while spending time with our beloved child makes us feel guilty. If we were a better parent, wouldn't we be delighted to spend every moment with our child? Morning Pages point out our feelings of self-pity. It is common for parents to experience these feelings. Throughout history, new parents were not isolated. Living in multigenerational households and tight-knit communities, new parents always had other adults around. Privacy and the nuclear family are relatively new phenomena, and come with both benefits and pitfalls.

A young father in my current Artist's Way workshop in Santa Fe began doing Morning Pages and quickly discovered that he was stuffing a lot of anger as a new parent.

"I'm embarrassed to say it," he confided in me. "But I envy my still-single friends. I can't go out with them anymore, I can't stay up late, and I feel like my life is never going to be fun again—at least in the way it was. I can't believe how jealous I am of their freedom."

"It's common to feel those feelings," I told him. But I suspected that there was more to it than just jealousy about their lifestyle.

"Is it that you miss them?" I prodded.

He sighed deeply. "Yes," he said. "I really miss them. I feel like they have almost turned against me. In a way, I need them more than ever now—and I feel like I have them less than ever."

Very often our single or childless friends are threatened by our new parental roles. They feel scared of, even competitive with our children. Used to having immediate access to us, they can be almost hostile when they don't get what they want from us because we are dealing with our kids.

"It may take a little creativity, but what about trying to bring your friends into your new family?" I asked him. "Is there a way you can imagine doing that?"

He thought for a moment, and then said, "You know, it's really simple, but the thing my buddies and I used to do is get together on Sunday afternoons and watch football. Maybe I'll invite them all over—like old times. If I have to be in the next room tending to the baby some of the time, so be it—I'd still like to have my friends in the house. And maybe they'd like to see what my new life really looks like."

A week later, he returned. "I had a football party," he grinned at me. "My wife and I took turns taking care of the baby. There were some moments when he cried and screamed, but my friends were surprisingly accepting of it. And some of them were just so taken with my son, wanting to hold him. The game was on in the other room, so people could do what they wanted to do. But I realized I haven't lost my friends. They just didn't know how to be a part of my new life. I just needed to invite them in."

As time went on, the young father found that he was able to continue his friendships with his "old" friends, and that he made new friends as well. Having kids opened the door to meeting other people with kids, and he found his circle became larger, not smaller, because of it.

The use of the three Basic Tools will guide us away from isolation, toward connection. It is pivotal that we as parents manage to retain our sense of adventure—and that parenting be considered an adventure. The key is to proactively find adventures that get us out of the house and interacting with other people. As we plan and execute outings, we become connected—to ourselves, our children, and the world around us.

ARTIST DATE

An Exercise

One of the basic tools of *The Artist's Way* is the Artist Date: a once-weekly, solo endeavor to do something fun, and alone. An Artist Date is not meant to be high art. It is simply to take yourself out on a "date" that sounds like an adventure you would enjoy.

List five outings that might be fun, such as visiting a bakery, getting a manicure with a wild fingernail color, visiting a garden store, going to a baseball game, and attending a concert.

1. _____
   _____
2. _____
   _____
3. _____
   _____
4. _____
   _____
5. _____
   _____

This week, hire a babysitter for two hours and take yourself on an Artist Date. Few things connect us to ourselves more than the willingness to take this simple outing.

(continued)

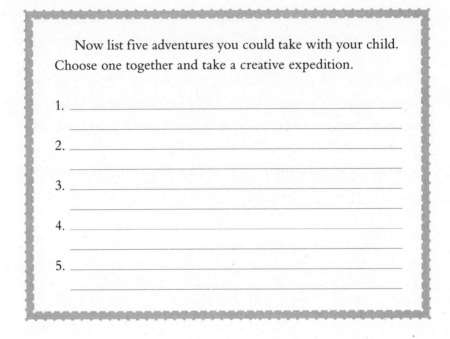

Now list five adventures you could take with your child. Choose one together and take a creative expedition.

1. _____
   _____

2. _____
   _____

3. _____
   _____

4. _____
   _____

5. _____
   _____

THE SAFETY CIRCLE

I remember once telling a friend of mine that I was lonely as a parent, only to realize that it was that friend's harsh judgment of me—and my admission of loneliness—that made me feel so alone. "Why would you be lonely," she asked pointedly, "when you are always with your daughter?" I realized there was a pervasive mythology around parenting. That mythology tells us we should be completely fulfilled by our children, and that if we aren't, there's something wrong with us. I had to survey my friends with a discerning eye. Some of them tried to make me feel ashamed of how I felt. It was a rare and valuable friend who could say to me, "Of course you're lonely. I'd be lonely, too." As we enter this new stage of life, our identity as well as our day-to-day routine is suddenly and drastically changed.

My career had been consuming, demanding and exciting, and it was a shock to me to find myself cast suddenly as "Mother." Somehow, engaged in my pregnancy, it never occurred to me that the baby would be my responsibility forever. But there it was. I was responsible, and my friends needed to adjust as well. Some of them found my new persona difficult to embrace. They missed their hard-drinking, tough-talking colleague. Others of my friends, Julianna McCarthy among them, provided a welcome strand of continuity, remembering the "old" me while welcoming the "new" me. I realized that what I needed to do was establish a "Safety Circle"—a cluster of friends with whom I could be wholly and candidly myself. I needed to surround myself with those who saw me as "Mommy," but not just as "Mommy." I needed to let go of some cherished friendships and find others that could take their place.

Some of my new friends were surprising. I'm thinking now of Blair. A confirmed bachelor and playboy, he unexpectedly demonstrated interest in and affection for my daughter. "I'll keep her for a couple of hours," he would volunteer, allowing me to make a dash to a bookstore or film, always feeling a little guilty that I was playing hooky, but increasingly aware that my windows of freedom were bearing fruit for me in terms of greater patience with my child.

A student of mine, Josh, found that by naming and thus becoming conscious of his own Safety Circle, he was able to better keep his clarity during times of stress. Josh, a lawyer, has a high-powered and time-consuming job in a corporate office. "It's up to me to provide for my family," he says. "But I am spending long hours away from home. My wife resents it, and I often feel like it's her and our son against me. I'm starting to feel like a stranger in my own house—like I'm not welcome there." Josh reached out to a member of his Safety Circle on his lunch break, confiding in his friend that he felt a rift growing with his wife. "Just telling my friend the truth was so liberating," says Josh. "I realized that my wife and I both felt lonely and overworked. And that I needed to reach out to both her and my son." Turning back to the Basic Tools, Josh took the time to check in with both his wife and child, asking them the highlights of their day. "I didn't really want to try it," he confessed, "but I promised myself I would do it, even if I was uncomfortable. I had been pushing her away as much as she had been pushing me away. And we both thought we were doing everything for the family. I think what we really needed was to listen to each other, support each other."

Our Safety Circle can include our spouse or partner, and keeping an open communication builds strength in our relationships with each other and our children. There is a healthy balance of together and alone time that we strive to achieve.

In our busy lives, many of us crave creative solitude. Few of us realize how even a little can go a long, long way. Karen and Doug have two beautiful children. Their boys are energetic and demanding. When Karen picks them up from day care, they have stories to tell, not all of them tattling on each other. Karen takes them home and settles them in the kitchen with a snack of cookies and milk. Next, she settles herself with a notebook and pen. Dating the page, she reviews her workday, taking care to note tasks well done. By the time her children have finished their snack, Karen has finished her check-in.

When Doug comes home, he will focus first on the kids and then on Karen. Dinner is family time, and after dinner, while Doug does the dishes, Karen bathes the kids. Once the kids have been put snugly to bed, they are both able to snatch fifteen minutes for themselves. This is time enough for Karen to take a restorative shower or make a phone call, and for Doug to relax with a magazine and his own thoughts. Karen and Doug then take time to check in with each other, making it a point to communicate honestly about where they are in the moment. Because they make their connection a priority, they are grounded and able to be present in their day, for themselves, each other, and their children.

Sally, a stay-at-home mom, admitted that she felt guilty about spending time with her Safety Circle. Because her husband earned the family income, she felt that he deserved to have the weekends to relax. But giving her husband the weekends left her on-duty 24/7. She hadn't any room for downtime in her own very demanding full-time job of raising their child. "I am a member of a bowling league," she told me. "We've gotten together every weekend since high school. It's my favorite activity and my favorite group of people. I can tell them anything. But what I've been telling them—and myself—now is that since I'm the first one of the group to have a child, I can no longer give up the time to bowl with them."

"Is there a day-care center at the bowling alley?" I asked Sally.

"Yes, but I can't leave Sharon there. I can't imagine putting her in day care just so I can hang out with my friends and bowl."

"I think you should try it," I urged her. "Just once. And see how you feel."

Sally came back, elated. "I don't know who had more fun!" she exclaimed. "Sharon was obsessed with the day care and is begging to go back. And I felt like I'd come home, seeing my friends again. It was a much needed break—and a much needed connection to a group of girls I know I can talk to."

Sally shared her excitement with her husband and he encouraged her to take a few hours for herself every weekend—and not just at a place where she could bring their daughter. "I'll take Sharon a few hours each weekend day," he suggested, "so you can have a little time for yourself in addition to your bowling." Seeing his wife's happiness at having a chance to connect with her friends inspired him to try to offer her more. And, as a bonus, he was able to have important one-on-one time with their daughter, as well. "I'm a parent, too," he told her, "and we all need for me to participate. It's good for everyone." At first Sally was unsure of how to spend her newfound windows of time, but she soon found that keeping up her friendships and independent interests was relaxing and rejuvenating, and ultimately gave her more energy as a spouse and as a parent.

As you look for your Safety Circle, you will find that there are some old friends and some new friends within it. It is important that the members of your Safety Circle be able to relate to all of the different parts of you. A quick check-in with people with whom you are able to be completely yourself can give you enormous energy. It is hard to underestimate the importance of just being heard.

BUILDING THE SAFETY CIRCLE
An Exercise

Make a list of people you can be totally honest with. Call one of them and check in—even for a few short minutes—every day.

DOWNTIME

"I have no time—like, really no time," new parents tell me. When we have children, our lives are no longer our own. Focused—rightfully—on providing for our children's many needs, we watch our own needs start to pile up like the unattended laundry. Over and over again, we resolve to "get to it later," charging on through our day, willing our anxieties away as we focus on what is "more important"—the child demanding our attention and energy.

"I love reading," says Todd, an editor. "I chose my career based on my love of books. Before I had children, I read a book a week, sometimes two. It is my greatest passion and my guiltiest pleasure. I read new manuscripts for my work and classics for my own enjoyment. My greatest inspiration comes from analyzing and appreciating how different writers choose to use the English language. I would almost call it a spiritual practice."

But today, as a father with two sons ages six and eight, Todd laments no longer having time to read as he pleases. "I haven't opened a classic since I had kids," he says. "I'm ashamed to admit it, but I resent that. I'm careful not to take my feelings out on my kids, but every time I look at the untouched book on my bedside table, it's another little reminder that there's no time for my interests anymore."

Deciding that there's "no time" for something we love is a thought that is well worth examining. If we decide that there is no time to read for pleasure—because it isn't important, because it would "only" make us happy—we are deciding that there is no time for ourselves, for our own spiritual balance, and we are making a dangerous decision indeed. Not only are we putting ourselves at risk of becoming resentful, we are modeling this behavior for our children.

"I come home from work and want to spend time with my kids," says Todd. Of course he does. But all children take naps when they are young, take movie breaks when they are older, become consumed in a project they are focusing on. The trick is to conserve our energy, grab the moments we can, and allow ourselves to spend them as we please.

The act of spending time doing something we *want* to do as opposed to something we *have* to do takes courage. Baby steps may be necessary here. Be gentle with yourself, and be willing to try something small.

Giving ourselves even fifteen minutes a day that is our own can turn our anxiety into optimism. Our children lie down for a nap, and we rush toward the dirty dishes, the unopened mail, the business calls that we haven't yet returned. We push our desires away as we push ourselves toward the imaginary finish line of being "done" with our ongoing list of "things to do." It has been said that the average person has two to three hundred hours of "things to do" to be "caught up." We will never be caught up. But we can adjust our course in small, daily ways to bring more balance into our lives. When we allow space for our own desires, we discover the unexpected paradox: by taking a "selfish" moment, we actually become more productive—and more available to our children.

"What book do you crave to read right now? For pleasure?" I ask Todd. He looks away, guilty that he craves this luxury, wishing he hadn't admitted it to me in the first place.

"*Moby Dick*," he says quietly. "But I've read it before. I don't really need to read it again. I'm so behind on everything else—it's ridiculous for me to waste time re-reading a book for no reason. My kids need me to be available to them."

"What do you love about *Moby-Dick*?" I prod. I myself have many favorite books that I have read over and over.

"Each time I read it, I see something new. The larger themes inspire me with their constant relevance. I feel connected somehow." Todd's eyes light up as he speaks.

"Great," I say. "You have to find fifteen minutes a day to read *Moby-Dick*. Giving yourself that gift is as important as anything else on your list. Just try it for a week and see what happens."

When Todd phones me a week later, his optimism is palpable. "I thought you were crazy," he says. "But because you challenged me to try this, I did. Maybe I wanted to prove you wrong—but whatever the reason, I'm so glad I tried it." I smile to myself, suspecting that his small, "selfish" act has made a big improvement in his week.

"First of all, I do have fifteen minutes every day," he tells me. "I could have promised you I didn't, but it turns out that I do. I might be sleepy, or stressed, or anxious, but in those moments I'm not that productive anyway." Todd is correct: when we are out of sorts, we are not at our best. Trying to cram a business e-mail into a hectic moment, we are impatient with requests and our impatience is the subtext of what we write. We copy someone we didn't mean to. We call someone by the wrong name. We hit "send" and then realize our error with horror. Meanwhile, we are not available to the child sitting next to us who wants us to look at their drawing or help them choose a shade of blue from the crayon box. Trying to do "one more thing," we do much less.

"I decided that for one week, I would try this," Todd says. "So, every day, when I thought I should do the dishes or get just a little more work done, I would pick up *Moby Dick*. At first I felt so guilty. I could hardly focus on it. But I said I would give it fifteen minutes a day, and I did. I found that within a few minutes, I was absorbed. And within a few days, I really looked forward to continuing where I left off.

"My younger son, Sam, was fascinated," Todd continues. "He wanted to know what I was reading, what the story was about. I told him I had read the book many times before, and that it gave me pleasure to read it again. I found myself being more patient and efficient at home and at work. I was excited to talk to Sam about the story, and it made me realize that when I was constantly running from one job to another, even when the job was something for my sons, I wasn't really available to talk to them anyway. To my surprise, no one seemed to mind that I was taking a moment for myself each day. I almost thought no one even really noticed, until I discovered Sam last night, sitting in my leather chair, feet up on my ottoman, with a book in his lap. When I asked him what he was reading, he replied, 'I'm reading a great book, Dad. It's about a whale.' He held up the book, showing me its cover: *Pinocchio*."

I hear Todd's voice waver slightly over the phone.

"You must have been proud," I say.

"I felt like a great father."

"Do you think you'll keep reading?" I ask, already knowing the answer.

"Absolutely," Todd laughs. "I am already thinking of which book I'll read next. It's amazing how giving this tiny gift to myself makes me more present during the rest of the day—and makes me a better parent."

When we are willing to make time for ourselves, willing to do the things that will make us happy, we give our children an enormous gift: the example of self-care. Taking pleasure in our true interests teaches them to do the same.

HEIGHTENING DOWNTIME
An Exercise

List ten "frivolous" things that make you happy but that you believe you no longer have time to do, such as cooking for yourself, listening to classical music, and knitting.

1. _____
   _____
2. _____
   _____
3. _____
   _____

(continued)

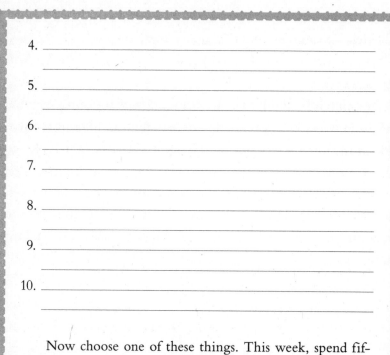

4. _____

5. _____

6. _____

7. _____

8. _____

9. _____

10. _____

Now choose one of these things. This week, spend fifteen minutes a day indulging in it. Fifteen minutes is a lot more than no minutes—and fifteen minutes is enough.

WHO YOU "WERE"

The shock of becoming a parent often leaves us feeling untethered, adrift, removed from life as we knew it. Who we "were" before we were parents feels like a distant and untouchable past. But there is a path back to ourselves, and we do not need to abandon our children to travel it.

Stephanie, a fitness instructor, recently had her first child. "I couldn't be more in love with Amelia," she gushes. "But I have to admit it's like the 'me' I once knew is not here anymore. I don't recognize myself, and to be honest, it really scares me."

An optimist by nature, Stephanie is a popular teacher as well as a personality in the fitness industry. She has created workout DVDs and has made her living professing the benefits of healthy living and scientific, structured exercise. Through her pregnancy, she continued to work out, blogging about her experiences and letting moms-to-be know that it was indeed safe to continue their fitness routines even into the ninth month of pregnancy. At the peak of fitness, Stephanie gave birth to a beautiful baby girl.

"I am afraid it's just vanity, but I am upset about how my body has changed," Stephanie confesses. "I'm exhausted, and I end up eating whatever is fastest—and that's not helping me get my body back, either. I know better. I know that when our bodies are tired, we can fool them by replacing sleep with food. It may give me temporary energy, but it's also making me fat." With her new, all-consuming daily routine with her daughter, and without the endorphins of exercise she had always maintained as an athlete, Stephanie felt her anxiety level starting to rise in a way she had not experienced before.

Stephanie is not alone in feeling like she has lost her "self" in more ways than one. When we become parents, we lose a part of our identity—gaining a joyful new one, but losing some of our freedom and sense of independence nonetheless. We must be very honest with ourselves: What are we willing—truly willing—to give up? What are we not willing to give up?

When Stephanie's daughter turned six months old, Stephanie made a change. "I realized I had to return to my workouts—tired or not, it is a part of me. It's my livelihood, but also my meditation, my source of strength. I bought one of those jogging strollers and started taking long walks every day with my daughter. Sometimes I would jog a little with her in her stroller. While my daughter napped, I popped in a DVD and did my own workout tapes next to her crib. I know how to get in shape. It was just a matter of doing it—making it a priority, like I always tell my students."

As Stephanie returned to her work and her workouts, her anxiety level diminished radically. "I got my body back, and I got my personality back, too. Looking in the mirror and seeing someone else was depressing and confusing. It distracted me from my daughter. I feel like I'm learning the lessons all over again that I myself teach—love your body, and it will love you back. I'm relaxed and optimistic when I push myself physically. I'm anxious and depressed when I don't. It's as simple as that—for me, I feel like the difference between doing my workouts and not doing them is the difference between being sane and being insane. And I want to be sane for my daughter," she adds, laughing.

Who you "were" is still a part of you. Although it may appear that there is no way to return to your former self, even the smallest steps in the direction of your desires will lead to greater energy and optimism.

Norah, a longtime student of mine and a Broadway actress, experienced great change in every part of her life when she became a parent. "I got married, got pregnant, and moved across the country when I met my husband, a studio executive," she remembered. "I was so grateful for my new life, but it was so different from the life I knew. Suddenly in a new city, away from my friends and career, and about to have a child, I felt panicked. I had worked so hard to be an actress, and it was what I loved to do. I no longer saw how I would be able to do it."

Norah had her child and, finding herself home most of the

time in a foreign place, fought pangs of sadness. "I didn't miss the life of sitting in New York, waiting for the phone to ring," she said. "But as I stood in my house in Los Angeles, changing diapers and looking out at the palm trees, I knew this life wouldn't be enough for me, either."

"I'm so far from New York now," she continued. "I didn't want to give up my acting career—I just wanted to add more to my life."

The fire of her dreams was not going to go out, and I told her as much. "Abandoning the stage isn't an option for you," I said to Norah. "But abandoning your family isn't an option either. You have to find a way to do both. Maybe you aren't up for a Broadway schedule right now, but there are other steps you can take."

"I've thought about writing a one-woman show," Norah confided to me. "But I've never written anything. I think of myself as just being an actress."

I felt immediately excited as she spoke. "Well, then," I encouraged her, "it sounds like you need to write." In my experience as a teacher, it is often the students who desire to write but don't think of themselves as writers who actually have the most to say.

"Do you really think I could do it?" Norah asked me, gently hopeful.

"I do. And remember—a show is written a page at a time, and all you have to worry about for now is a first draft. Editing and rewriting can happen later. Producing it can happen much later. Just try to put pen to page and let yourself express what you are going through."

A week later at class, Norah was excited to give me an update. "I have been writing—just a little every day while Cooper naps, but I have ten pages already! I find myself thinking about my life differently, knowing I am going to write it down. I watch myself with more compassion, as if I am creating a narrative through my day. Today I even had an idea for a song."

Norah is a brilliant woman, and I can't help thinking that her foray into writing may give her career longevity that she might never have expected. Because she was willing to act on her dream, even for just a few minutes a day, she was able to experience a shift in perspective—on herself and on her life—that ultimately brought her greater happiness. And yes, three years later, Norah did a short New York run of her one-woman show—about an actress with a child—adding the titles of writer, composer, and producer to her already impressive résumé.

As you see your life change, please be gentle with yourself. You do not have to abandon yourself to be a parent. Becoming a parent leads you to a new life, a life that has room for an expansive you that contains both the old and the new.

Ann, a mother of four grown children, recalls her own experience of, as she named it, "losing myself to find myself." Ann was a model before she had children, and when she became a mother, she no longer had the same opportunities available to her. "I was at home, and I felt like I had lost my identity as I knew it. I couldn't model anymore, and that was what I had spent the last ten years of my life doing."

Ann decided that, just for fun, she would create a class for girls in her suburban Chicagoland community. Naming the class "Beauty Inside and Out," Ann taught girls about taking care of themselves—on the inside and the outside—building confidence and poise as they learned to stand up straight, keep their hair out of their faces, and use discernment with makeup colors and application. As Ann worked with her students, directly addressing the specific ways in which they could best carry themselves through the world physically, she was interested—and delighted—to see that they became more personally self-assured, as well.

"Every girl thinks about how she looks," says Ann. "If her bangs are in her eyes, she is trying to cover something up. It's always related, the inside and the outside. I'm convinced of it." As Ann, with her gentle candor, helped her young students, she realized that the wisdom she was imparting was deeply empowering to them.

"I think I assumed that modeling was superficial," Ann muses. "But I realized that what I could teach girls was really valuable." Twenty years later, Ann is still teaching "Beauty Inside and Out." And when Ann's fourth child went to college, she became a modeling agent, teaching poise and confidence to her clients, as well.

In our society we have such a powerful archetype of "mother" that it doesn't occur to people that you have any other role. In remembering who you "were," it is very helpful if you have a friend with whom you can keep continuity, a friend who knew you as you were, but is also open to knowing you as you now are. Some of your friends from "before" will not be comfortable with your evolution, and you must also make an effort to find new friends in your new role. When you do, filling them in on the historical you—and learning about who they "were," too—can help you to feel connected to your past and present life, both of which are relevant and valuable to your parenting and to your child.

WALKING

An Exercise

There is little that moves us more quickly into clarity than walking. As we redefine our identity to include "parent," it is important to venture out into fresh air and let the simple, meditative act of walking help us to process our new role and our new self. Take yourself on a twenty-minute walk with your child. The walk should have no agenda. Simply getting out into nature is enough. Allow yourself to take in the sights and sounds. When you return, take pen to page. Did any insights come to you as you walked?

Chapter Two

CULTIVATING CURIOSITY

~

Children explore the world with wonder. They have an inherent curiosity facing each day as they eagerly and inquisitively uncover the new and discover the unexpected. Our job as parents is to facilitate their exploration. By valuing and trusting their playtime, we value and trust their unique and creative perspective. By providing raw materials with which to explore their many and varied ideas and interests, we allow their imaginations to take flight. Our job is to encourage them with interest, and even take a cue from their playful endeavors. Resisting the urge to "direct" their play, we lighten up— and light up. There is hardly a greater gift to a child than a parent whose own sense of curiosity is delightfully in bloom.

GETTING SERIOUS ABOUT PLAY

In my book *The Artist's Way*, I routinely encourage adults to "play." Recovering our childlike sense of wonder makes us happier, more productive adults. Many of the exercises I take my adult students through have to do with remembering fond moments from our childhood when we felt free to create with abandon.

And now it is up to us to ensure that our children will have these memories when they grow older. In a culture that is only getting busier, faster, and more technological, the pressure falls on parents to protect their children's sense of wonder and give them the space to develop it.

One of my fondest memories as a child was the music that seemed to always flow through our house. Our family home had two pianos: one in the living room for formal play, and one in the playroom for "fooling around." "Fooling around"—experimenting and playing "just for fun"—builds a sense of confidence in our children and a sense of faith in a benevolent Universe where their creative ideas are welcome. When they are allowed to play "just for fun," they are allowed to make mistakes. "Do not fear mistakes; there are none," said Miles Davis. Taking this attitude with our children—that their creativity is not a performance but an inherent part of who they are—we teach them that it is safe to take chances. As we encourage their exploration by praising their creative whims, they continue to grow, experiment, and take risks in all aspects of their lives.

"My daughter is three years old," says David. "She lives in fantasy right now. Sometimes if she's playing in her room, I'll stand in the doorway for a minute until I understand 'where she is.' The other day I saw her sobbing on her bed as she told a story to her stuffed animals. I didn't interrupt her, I just listened. Within a short amount of time, I realized that she was telling a story where Jafar had just killed Aladdin. When she finished recounting the tragedy to her toys, she wiped her eyes and started up on something else. What I find remarkable is that she is so creatively uninhibited right now. I want to protect that in her."

I believe that there are fewer things more important than protecting this sense of wonder in our children. As long as our children feel safe to experiment, they are developing into original thinkers.

The playroom piano in the Cameron house was painted white and gold—and we kids did that painting. Our musical play was encouraged by our mother. "See if you can play 'Silent Night,'" she would say with a smile. And when we did, "See if you can play 'Twinkle, Twinkle, Little Star.'" Often we would pick our melodies out by ear. Sometimes two of us would share the piano bench. "You'll have to play that for your father," my mother would exclaim when we had triumphantly picked out a melody. I remember the thrill of finding a melody within the keys, and the excitement in my mother when I did. Today, decades later, I have written hundreds of melodies that I picked from the keys with much the same curiosity. Always, I have a piano in my home. Daily, I write on it.

Play is important for all ages. I would argue that we never reach an age where play isn't productive.

"Productive? Really, Julia?" my students counter. "Even though I struggle just to get the kids fed, bathed, and to bed at a decent hour?"

Yes. Even though there is never "enough" time, carving out

time for play is essential. It doesn't have to be much time—really, any amount of time will do. But children who play freely then go through life with a playful attitude, a levity that helps them deal with harder situations. I believe that adults who make time for play are consistently more creative and effective in their lives as well. Allowing ourselves to play, we connect to a sense of inner wonder and safety—in other words, a sense of faith.

Jill, a former lawyer, turned into a stay-at-home mom when her son was born. "I didn't need money," she told me. "I didn't have to work. So I stayed home. I thought I was being a better parent by giving my son all of me, everything I had."

Well-intentioned and formidably intellectual, Jill found herself frustrated during her son's childhood. As her marriage crumbled, her focus on her child became more intense. Not using her own talents, she became obsessed with his. No longer writing for law journals, she wrote her son's papers instead. His education became her business. His test scores were high, but she wanted them higher. His grades were high, but "not quite high enough"— meaning not as high as hers had been.

"Do you let your son play?" I asked her.

"He plays violin and soccer," she replied. "He plays tennis three times a week with a renowned coach." That wasn't exactly what I had meant by "play." Although he was on a top soccer team, he didn't seem passionate about soccer. He showed up at his tennis lessons without enthusiasm. He practiced his violin, but only under Jill's strict orders.

And was her son happy? In fact, at age twelve, he had many behavioral issues that weren't improving as time passed. Jill hired specialists, tutors, psychologists. But at the core, things didn't change. His teachers were at a loss, he was antisocial, and he often fought with his mom.

"I wonder if you could try giving him some free time to play," I suggested to Jill. "Just a little."

"How?" she scoffed defiantly. "How do I do that, and how is it going to help? He's already been to France twice this year. That was a vacation."

"No, not expensive vacations," I offered gently. "Just time to do nothing. Time to do whatever he wants. Not play with video games or on the computer, but to explore something new on his own. It should cost nothing. Give him an hour."

Visibly uncomfortable, Jill glared at me. She hated my suggestion. Her son never did anything without her watching.

"What I actually think," I told Jill, "is that you should both have an hour just to play. You can both be at home, but just give each other some space—you in one room, him in another. Give it a try. Just once, as an experiment."

Reluctantly, Jill agreed. Approaching her son, she asked him if he'd like to take an hour alone to do something fun at home. Anything he wanted. His eyes narrowed. "Why?" he asked suspiciously. "What's the agenda? Are you going to be watching me?"

"I'm not going to be watching you," Jill promised. "I'm going to be in my room, relaxing."

"That's not true," her son countered. "You never relax."

"I know," Jill admitted. "But I'm going to try it. And you can try it, too. And we'll see how we both liked it at the end of the hour."

"I don't have to be doing homework?" he asked her.

"You don't have to be doing homework. I'd prefer that you

not watch TV or play on the computer—no screens for an hour. But other than that, it's up to you."

Jill went to her room. She glanced at the clock, plucked a book from the shelf that she'd read for pleasure years before, and settled herself in her corner chair.

Meanwhile, her son entered his room cautiously. Could it really be true that he was allowed to do anything he wanted? For a whole hour? He glanced at the computer on his desk. The only rule is not to use screens, he thought. He felt a little thrill of adventure. If not the computer, then what did he want to do? So often the computer was an escape for him—an escape from his mother's prying eyes and iron grip, to be specific—that he almost resented it. The computer was a hiding place. It was a place to retreat to when he didn't want to interact with his mother, when he didn't want to talk to the other kids at school. It wasn't exactly a good place. Looking around his bedroom, he noticed a collection of toy robots that he had been given years before, for his sixth birthday, before his parents divorced. He had become blind to them, but there they were, sitting on his shelf where they had been for years. After pulling them out, he played for a minute with the toys he had outgrown, remembering a different time—a time when his family had been intact. Then he moved to his desk and took a legal pad and a pencil from his drawer and began to write.

Meanwhile, Jill was shocked to see how quickly time had passed. Looking up from her book, it had already been an hour and fifteen minutes, and she hadn't heard a sound from her son's room. Walking quietly toward his door, she glanced inside. He sat, brow furrowed, writing on his legal pad, oblivious to her presence. Swallowing an excited exclamation, she moved back down the hall to the kitchen, where she started to prepare dinner.

"It was amazing," Jill told me later. "Truly amazing. That night at dinner he told me he had written a short story about a boy living in Boston. It was clear that the story was about him, but I didn't let on that I knew that. He's had a hard time since his father and I got divorced, and I've so often tried to get him to talk about it. He's always disappearing into his computer instead. But the fact that he's writing—I was moved to tears. And we had more to talk about that night at dinner than we had in a long time." As Jill continued to give herself and her son these "free" hours on an almost daily basis, she was thrilled to see his grades and demeanor start to improve as well.

"There's a lot he can figure out on his own, I guess," she told me sheepishly. "I thought I had to have all the answers. But I don't have them."

I say, thank God we don't. And remembering that we are, in-deed, not God frees us and our children to access the divine creative spirit within each of us—and to be surprised and de-lighted by what we find. Following our creative urgings, we learn there is only one thing we can expect: the unexpected. And there is little more thrilling than experiencing this gentle sense of surprise.

Play is important for all ages. Allowing ourselves—and our children—play time unlocks a certain magic in all of us, regard-less of age or intellect. When we let our children's play run its course, when we resist hovering and meddling with what they are doing, or putting so much pressure on product that the idea of process is lost, we and our children are truly free.

REDISCOVERING PLAY
An Exercise

If you find yourself wanting to hover over your children and micromanage their play, you might need more play yourself. Can you give yourself—and your child—the gift of letting go? It may be as simple as letting your toddler explore drawing without "improving" their artwork, or letting him tell you a story without finishing it for him.

Take pen in hand and list five ways that you played during your own childhood. Choose fond memories. How exactly did you feel? Free, open, safe? Now choose one of these activities and create the space for your child to do the same thing.

Example:

I felt free when I was allowed to "perform" an original story for my parents. I would create a stage in the middle of the living room, make a grand entrance, and tell a story. All they did was laugh and applaud. I can give this experience to my child today by setting that "stage," asking her to tell a story, and doing nothing myself except enjoy the show.

I felt free when _____. I could give that experience to my child today by _____.

I felt free when _____. I could give that experience to my child today by _____.

I felt free when _____. I could give that experience to my child today by _____.

> I felt free when _____. I could give that experience to my child today by _____.
>
> I felt free when _____. I could give that experience to my child today by _____.

RAW MATERIALS

I grew up in a house that was well stocked with play materials. We had building blocks, LEGO, clay, crayons, acrylic paints, and musical instruments. All of these resources were available to us "on demand." We had coloring books and blank paper for free-form drawing. Our mother would set out the day's choice of supplies. Sometimes she would suggest a topic, for example, "Today, let's draw horses," or "Today, let's draw kitties." And so we would set our hand to rendering what was chosen. Our mother would leave us to our own devices, checking in on us every so often.

Our playroom had a vinyl floor, so our messes were easily cleaned up. Sometimes, one of us would do a particularly fine drawing and our mother would exclaim over its excellence, asking, "Can I pin this up?" She had a large bulletin board where she posted our finest work. Sometimes our work would be so wonderful that it deserved framing. This was something our father undertook. It was thrilling to have a piece of our art framed and hung on the wall. I still remember my sense of pride when they chose to frame a rearing golden palomino horse I'd drawn, complete with mountains in the background.

The very definition of creation—making something from

nothing—is an ability that we all have, but young children may be the most in touch with it. Worlds are created from a blank page and a few colored pencils. Stories are written as plastic horses gallop across the tiles on the kitchen floor.

Children are playful, and they will play with the materials they have at hand. If nothing else is available, they'll play with sticks and dirt. Pots, pans, and spoons are excellent playthings.

"I say don't buy toys," says Linda, a mother of three. "You're always going to have plenty of toys, given as gifts or inherited. There's never a shortage of toys. And definitely don't buy a toy that has only one use—because that's how many times it will be used: once. The best toys have a million uses. Blocks are my favorite."

Toys can make our homes into obstacle courses when we indulge in purchasing every toy of the moment, and keeping up with the fads is ultimately a lot less valuable than giving long-lasting tools to our children that allow them ample room for imagination.

We needn't go out and buy things. As parents, it falls to us to supply a variety of raw materials for creativity—the simpler, the better. The first and perhaps most powerful tool is blank paper. Just think of what a piece of blank paper can become: a drawing, a poem, a boat, a magic carpet—the possibilities are vast. The simple addition of a box of crayons entices your child into coloring. The finished drawing or tepee or hat should be given a place of honor. Your child is encouraged by the attention paid to his work. A few dress-up clothes can inspire your child to transform into characters, inventing stories and even performing made-up skits for the family or just for their toy collection.

Stuffed animals are another rich source of play. A few encouraging comments, such as "Is it Bunny's naptime?" will lead the child in fruitful directions. Stuffed animals may play together, and don't be surprised if your child creates a voice-over. Miniature farm animals, woodland creatures, plastic bugs can become imaginary environments where entire worlds exist.

Clay allows your child to work in three dimensions. Mommy, Daddy, household pets—all may be sculpted. Building blocks entice your child to create houses for their clay animals, or they may create a garage, which in turn requires toy cars to join in the fantasy.

Inviting your child to make music is a potent source of fun. A drum can be made of an empty oatmeal container. A tiny keyboard can be a source of great joy. Add tambourines, maracas, and a train whistle and you're ready for a parade.

The best toys are the most open-ended ones. Fertile play encourages concentration and focus, and, deep "in the zone" of play, our children often become so absorbed that they don't even notice that we're there. They are developing their ability to sustain attention. They are also developing their creativity.

My daughter, Domenica, preferred her herd of Breyer horses to any other form of play. She would "gallop" her herd from bedroom to living room. As she grew older, her play grew more complex. Her horses acquired names and distinct personalities. Two of her horses, Goldie the palomino and Sandy the Arabian, often vied for leadership of the herd.

"What about Spotty?" I would inquire, singling out her Appaloosa.

"No, Mommy," she would reply firmly, identifying the palomino as her leader of choice. Children are inventive, and the imaginary worlds they create are very real to them.

"I can give my four-year-old daughter, Sadie, a vacuum cleaner hose and she'll be occupied for a really impressive stretch of time," says Ronald, a writer. "It's amazing to me what she can do with nothing, really. I sit nearby, working on my book, and tear a page out of my notebook for her. Before I know it, Sadie tells me she is writing her own book. I feel like kids live so close to inspiration." Indeed. Inspiration and imagination may be much more closely related than we might at first realize. The willingness to look outside ourselves, to reach into the ethers and pull back whatever idea floats nearby, is a state that children live in, and a state that adults tend to move further from as the demands of their lives require them to be "sensible." But we are better off when we are imaginative, and our children are no different. Handing our children less is sometimes more: a vacuum cleaner hose may very well catapult Ronald's daughter into originality and freedom, while overcomplicated toys—or too many toys, period—may dampen her spark more than ignite it.

"I've learned the hard way that the more expensive and complex the toy is, the sooner my son loses interest in it," says Andi. "I think that giving him less really is more. The blank page never wears out for him. He'll do a million drawings with his old, dull crayons and ignore the elaborate remote-controlled car I spent too much money on. I think it's that whenever he is making something, he's always interested." When our children have room to grow, they fill that space. They want to grow. It is human nature to explore and expand. By handing them the raw materials that facilitate that, we encourage and enable their growth.

"But that's much too simple!" wails Gillian, a highly trained archaeologist. "You don't understand. I want my son to be brilliant. I want to teach him everything."

Yes, of course she does. But this assumes that Gillian knows everything. As parents, we often wish that we had the power to give—and teach—our children everything they could possibly need to know. And although this would be convenient in theory, it is neither true nor desirable.

As Gillian knows from her experience as an archaeologist, the fun is in the search. She never knows where her explorations will lead, and it is in this not-knowing that she is inspired to continue. The best raw materials we can give our children are the ones that allow the most room for their unique personalities to explore and expand.

For her daughter's sixth birthday party, Martha decided that instead of buying party favors available at the local dime store, she would create an activity for the girls at the party that would result in them going home with a party favor—but one that they had made themselves. At each girl's place at the table waited a brown paper bag. Also serving as a place card, each bag was decorated with a brightly colored sticker and featured the name of the guest in large, fancy print. Once at the table, the girls opened the bags to discover only raw materials inside: a wooden spool and some yarn. Martha showed the girls how the spool was built to weave a bracelet from the yarn in their bag. She showed them how to begin and helped them along as the girls each wove themselves a simple bracelet. At the end of the party, they each proudly wore their creations. Years later, the guests still remembered that party as being magical. "I made so many more bracelets with my spool," says Amy. "I taught my younger sister how to do it, too. In hindsight, the magic was in the feeling of creation. It was one of my favorite birthday parties I ever went to. I was always intimidated when there was a piñata, because it felt like a competition. But this

was so welcoming to everyone. We had something to bring home that we were proud of."

SOMETHING FROM NOTHING
An Exercise

Take pen in hand and list three "tools for exploration" that are already in your house. Are they being used regularly, or have they been dismissed? The simplest tools are best, and often inexpensive and already at hand.

1. _____

_____

2. _____

_____

3. _____

_____

Offer your child one of these items and allow yourself to be surprised at what you both might be able to make of it. And whatever you both make—appreciate it.

RESISTING THE URGE TO MEDDLE

Letting our children grow is much like planting a garden. We plant the seeds that we think will bring beauty to the world, survive the seasons, and continue to blossom fully, far past the moment we put them in the ground. But once we plant the seeds, we need to go on with our day, planting other seeds, attending to other tasks. If we obsessively watch the garden, waiting impatiently for our first green sprout, we will drive ourselves crazy, and, I would argue, slow our garden's progress.

The same is true for our children. We can suggest games, toys, and ideas, but it is not up to us what our children do with the suggestions we offer. As with the garden, we cannot hover over our children's delicate process and expect that it will help or speed it up. It is, in fact, likely to do the opposite.

When I teach, I often talk about how I am Johnny Appleseed, tossing out ideas and tools for growth and then going on my way. Behind me, my students grow and blossom. There is little that's more rewarding than seeing what happens when a person unlocks his or her own ideas and brings them to fruition. Our children are no different. We can offer suggestions as starting points, but what our children do with those suggestions is where the magic begins. The surprise lies in the inspiration that emerges. It may be moments later or years later, but it certainly feels like the work of God's hand when we observe the garden of our children's world start to grow.

As parents, we are as much a place for our child as a person. We are the place that is safe and secure. We provide a supportive atmosphere where our children are able to play. A day's play might begin by our setting out the day's tools—we might lay out an oilcloth, a tablet, and acrylic paints. We might lay out a small herd of toy horses. Our children might request the toys of the day, perhaps building blocks or modeling clay.

Once we have selected the day's playful paraphernalia, we can leave our children to their own devices. If we hover too close, we squelch our children's creativity. With the best of intentions, we can overdo our supervision. Let's say your child chooses to make a bright green dog. Your job is not to "correct" it; although you might say, "I've never seen a green puppy," you cannot say, "Puppies aren't green." Left alone to play with clay, your child may model a horse, or perhaps a lizard. Your job is to encourage it—whatever it is—and remind your child (and yourself) that there is no wrong way to play.

"When my son was born, I became 'that guy,'" Jake, an engineer, told me. "My dad was overbearing. I swore I would never be. But once I had a son of my own, it was like my conditioning took over. It wasn't about logic anymore. I named him Jake Junior, and immediately saw myself in everything he did. When he was three, I wanted to 'help' him put his puzzles together and, of course, ended up doing them for him. My perfectionistic attention to detail helps me in engineering, but not in parenting. It's like I thought it was my job to correct everything Jake Junior was doing, even when he was playing."

Inevitably, Jake Junior began to resist his father's meddling. At age three, he threw a tantrum when his dad impatiently put the simple puzzle together for his son. By age six, Jake Junior described his dad as "usually in a bad mood" and as someone who "tells people what to do."

"I realized I was turning into my father," Jake Senior continued. "And I had to think it through. I practically disowned my father by the time I was eighteen. And I had been resenting him for years before that. I didn't want this to happen to me and my son."

"What did you want from your father?" I prodded Jake.

"I wanted him to accept me. I wanted him to think I was good enough. When he did everything for me, I felt like he was showing me that he didn't have any faith that I could do it myself."

"Then maybe you can consciously look for ways to show Jake Junior that you accept him as he is. That you want to hear what he has to say. That his attempts and instincts matter. That you'll give him a chance to respond on his own."

Jake Senior reluctantly agreed to give it a try. After a few weeks, I heard from him again.

"I still have this voice inside telling me that by involving myself with everything my son does, I am helping him. But intellectually I know that I am being controlling by doing that. It was so hard for me to back off—and I failed in most of my early attempts. But one day, Jake Junior exploded at me. He was working on a model airplane, and he had made a mistake in building it. I corrected the mistake, and finished up the building of it. I thought he'd be excited to see that it was done, but he couldn't have been more upset. His face turned crimson, and through tears of frustration, he said, 'All of my projects become yours, Dad. You don't leave anything for me. You're mean.' I was totally taken aback. But then I realized that he couldn't have been more right.

"Even though I have provided a pretty luxurious life for my son, I have been stingy with him emotionally. And it occurred to me that every time I felt the need to control his action, thought, or reaction, maybe I should try giving him a compliment instead. And so every time I would think about correcting his homework, I'd look at something he had already done right and tell him I was proud of him for that. And then I'd leave the room. It felt like a totally radical experiment, but the results amazed me. He's been a lot more productive on his own. I'm realizing I can't control him—and I shouldn't. But I can improve the situation by adjusting my own behavior. And it does seem to trickle down."

Jake's story is, to my eye, an incredible leap forward. For Jake, letting go of his position as "boss" felt like losing his identity. Parenting is not the same as running a business. There may be interpersonal dynamics and strategic planning involved in both, but the same animal they are not.

When our children are young and we cannot venture too far from them, it is still possible to give them space to explore. Linda tells the story of her mother keeping toys on a special shelf in the kitchen. "She would be cooking dinner, and we would be on the kitchen floor, lost in our own world. She was doing what she needed to do, but she had an eye on us." When Linda had children, she built a toy cabinet in the kitchen. "We can all be near each other without being overly enmeshed. Everyone's safe, and everyone's being productive. And the sense of company is really nice."

When I was little, I preferred acrylic paints to crayons. While I labored away at painting a horse, my mother took advantage of my concentration to do some concentrating of her own. Seated at her writing desk, which was near—but not too near—our play area, she penned letters to her mother-in-law, Mimi, and to her far-flung siblings. She might comment on our play, but she wouldn't interrupt it.

Our children are aware of us, and they are aware when we are focused on them. They can sense when we trust their time alone and their individual flow of ideas. Sensing our trust, they learn to trust themselves. They allow themselves to venture down an imaginary road that brings them to a new idea and a sense of fulfillment and accomplishment. As time passes, these same skills will help them to become creative, confident thinkers.

In the Cameron home, our play often sought to integrate our

experience. "Look, Mom. It's Misty of Chincoteague." We were seeking to illustrate the novel by Marguerite Henry that was read to us at night. We might draw a choo-choo train toiling up a steep hill. "Look, Mom. The Little Engine That Could," we would announce.

It falls to us as parents to receive our children's offerings with delight. The more enthusiasm we can muster for their efforts, the more they will try. "Close but not too close" is the motto for this phase of our children's development. Sometimes I think of a parent as a lovely willow tree where children may play in the shade. I tried sharing this image with my daughter, who responded by making a crayon sketch of a tree with a child underneath. "That's me," she said proudly. "That's me," I echoed, pointing to the tree. "Oh, Mommy, you're not a tree," Domenica protested. "Sure I am," I said. "Just pretend."

Domenica did pretend, putting a tree in all her drawings.

Children who are allowed to be creatively free tend to become creatively free adults. And children whose play is discouraged or controlled tend to grow into people who second-guess their own instincts. It is a long path of recovery to regain that faith, and while not impossible, it is rigorous. I have watched thousands of my students work to recover their true identities as adults. It is exciting, fulfilling work. But if certain wounds can be avoided in the first place, isn't it our duty to try to prevent them?

As we trust and encourage our children to follow their imaginings wherever they may lead, we empower them to develop into original, creative beings. And there is little more magical, or more surprising, than watching their journey unfold.

DEFINING INTERESTS
An Exercise

Take pen in hand. List five of your favorite interests.

1. _____

2. _____

3. _____

4. _____

5. _____

Now list five interests your child has that you are unfamiliar with. Can you consciously let those interests be his alone, and allow those interests to blossom?

1. _____

2. _____

3. _____

4. _____

5. _____

THE POWER OF PRETEND

Goethe said, "Whatever you think you can do or believe you can do, begin it. Because action has magic, grace, and power in it."

I believe that every person is creative and that, as adults, we tend to stray from some of the natural inclinations we were born with. As we watch our children play, we remember a playful side of ourselves. As we see our children pretending, we remember our own sense of wonder and possibility. Inspiration lies in the mysterious, in the tiny flash of an idea that whispers to us, quietly inviting us to listen.

I believe that in our natural, unblocked state, we are in touch with this quiet voice. Children are naturally unblocked and naturally alert to these promptings. One of the most awe-inspiring things to witness, and one of the most powerful games to encourage in our children, is the game of pretend. They may play pretend with their friends, with their stuffed animals, alone, or with you. Imaginary friends are commonplace. Your child may carry on a long and winding conversation with this unseen companion, and your job is to step aside and allow them to "visit."

Patt tells the story of her son, Arthur, who, at age six, began his obsession with fairy tales. "I was just doing the dishes and watching the kids through the window," Patt says with a laugh, "and there was Arthur in the backyard with his Big Wheel flipped upside down. He was spinning the wheel with his hands so intently. He looked a little crazy, but he was having fun and he was safe, so I didn't bother to go outside and ask what he was doing. Then the next day, there he was doing it again." Patt shakes her head at the memory. "I had to know what was going on in that head of his. And when I asked him—get this—he said he was Rumpelstiltskin, spinning gold."

Patt smiles at the memory. "He was always very creative. Still is. His imagination is just always going like that. It's who he is. So who am I to get in the way?" Arthur went on to write musical adaptations of fairy tales, and quickly thereafter, to create his own fairy tales. By the age of twenty-five, he had written eight original full-length musicals.

"I am absolutely sure that spinning gold on the Big Wheel was connecting things in his brain," says his writing partner. "His understanding and knowledge of fairy tales is awesome. He thought about them so much that they are a part of his vocabulary, an almost automatic part of how his mind works today. I don't think there's anything better he could have been doing with his time. He is a genius for sure, but maybe more important than that is his enthusiasm. He loves what he does—and that's what makes him so productive. He is a fountain of energy because he is having fun."

Arthur's imagination is as alive today as it was the day he spun gold in the backyard, and when I look at Patt's parenting, I see why Arthur is so free as an artist. Patt's impulse as a parent was to encourage each of her four children along the lines of their interests and personalities. Today, she has four strikingly different—and staggeringly accomplished, kind, and personable—grown children. As I watch her interact with them now, I see hints of what she must have done all along. She loves them unconditionally, supports their ideas, has a keen interest in each, and puts none of them on a pedestal. Humor runs high in her household. Even today, as I talk with her about Rumpelstiltskin, she laughs. "I don't see myself as particularly creative, at least not in the way

Arthur is," she tells me. "But he's entertaining, that's for sure." As Patt continues to be a loving and enthusiastic audience member, she is giving Arthur everything he needs. Sometimes the right non-action is every bit as valuable as the right action: by not putting a lid of judgment or limits on his imaginative nature, Patt allowed Arthur to achieve his full potential with a feeling of safety and acceptance. Now an adult, Arthur also teaches, encouraging his students to explore freely. "The crazier, the better," he tells them.

Every game of pretend is valuable. Playing pretend allows our children a specific freedom, a safe space in which they can test out different personas and figure out which feels most comfortable to them. And when they leave that safe space, they leave with knowledge—self-knowledge, however subtle, that will contribute to their confidence in—and contribution to—the world at large.

DOLL-MAKING
An Exercise

Making a doll—any kind of doll—can be a cathartic and exciting exercise for both girls and boys. It does not need to be a traditional-looking doll, although it may be. Allow your child to choose his materials and create his doll by his own design. Making a doll is an ideal way to merge an arts-and-crafts project with pretend play. As your child is making the doll, be it from paper, a sock, a stick, or LEGO, interact

(continued)

with your child. Does the doll have a name? Where does this doll live? How old is it? Is it from the city or the country? Allowing the doll to have its own backstory gives your child ownership over its invention. Ask your child to tell you about this doll, and listen with openness. If the child gives the doll the same characteristics he has, he may be using the doll to consolidate his sense of self. If the child gives the doll very different characteristics, he may be exploring alternate personas. As a parent, your job is simply to observe with interest—and watching your child work with this exercise promises to be fascinating, indeed.

Chapter Three

CULTIVATING CONNECTION

⌒

G iving our children a safe hatchery allows them to con-nect securely to the world around them. Nature invites our children to experience a sense of connection. Flora and fauna bring to our children a feeling of companionship. The simple act of going outside and walking connects us to ourselves, one another, and the world around us. The universe is generous in its support of creative growth, and the more we actively look for this support, the more we will find. Expressing our gratitude for this support, we experience a sense of God—be it "good, or-derly direction" or a benevolent higher power—and experiencing this sense of the greater unknown, we connect to and become a part of it.

FLORA

I have often defined God with a Dylan Thomas verse: "The force that through the green fuse drives the flower." There is magic in the ongoing life in nature, in its resilience and unlimited rainbows of color and design. Exposing our children to nature in any form ignites their imagination and connects them to the endless potential of the natural world. I would argue that a connection to the natural world is also a connection to God, and to ourselves.

Connecting to nature can be very simple—as simple as just going outdoors. If you live in the country, the rich forests are deep with stories and magic, and the open plains are a blank canvas of possibility for your child's eyes. Planting a garden can give a sense of ownership and rebirth. If you live in the city, visiting the park or even the local flower shop can connect you and your child to the same force of nature. Window boxes and indoor plants expose both of you to the wonder of growth and seasonal cycles. Connecting to life and recognizing the many ways it surrounds us nourishes our creative spirit and our children's.

Courtney speaks of growing up in suburban Wisconsin, where her neighbors had blackberry bushes surrounding their property. Courtney and her sisters would pick blackberries in the summer, often wearing snowsuits in the heat to protect themselves from the thorns. They would return home, clothes and hands stained with the purple nectar, filled with excitement about their bounty.

"My four sisters and I have a twelve-year age range," Courtney says, "but all ages participated in the blackberry picking. It was like a treasure hunt. The treasure was sweet and delicious.

We'd often come home and our mother would help us bake them into blackberry muffins, bringing them back to the elderly couple who lived in the house next door. It was such a luxury to have the homemade muffins in the house, and the neighbors were so excited to let us pick the berries and so grateful to enjoy the final product. In hindsight, I realize that our neighbors were actually quite poor. As the years went on, they struggled a lot. But the blackberries were free and, picking blackberries, we all were rich."

Courtney and her sisters all fondly remember the blackberry-picking expeditions. All of them have the blackberry muffin recipe in their recipe boxes. Courtney herself went on to become a pastry chef. Her signature item? The blackberry turnover.

"It has a history for me," she says. "And I'm sure that my own connection to the blackberries at the Hardys' house is why this pastry is so popular. They say you can 'taste the love'—and I do think that's true. For me, picking blackberries was about more than that. It was about sisterhood, adventure, feeling welcomed by the Hardys, baking with my mother. I've picked a lot of blackberries in my day. I can tell by sight which ones are the sweetest."

Courtney's pastries do evoke the memories she based the recipe on. Her customers report that the soft, flaky texture and sweet, deep purple filling give them a feeling of comfort and hospitality.

Gardening can be a fascinating joint effort for you and your child. Vegetable gardens that ultimately yield salad fixings or herbs, or flowers that grow from seed to blooming plant under your watchful eye, can teach patience and attention.

Mary, an avid gardener, was known on her suburban Indiana block for her sprawling, colorful flower beds. "Pansies are my favorite," she told me. "I love their saturated colors, and they're practically invincible." When her grandchildren would visit, she would take them to the backyard, where they would select a few of the thriving beauties. Cutting them carefully with scissors, she would bring them inside and show her grandchildren how to press the flowers by flattening them gently between paper towels, and then weighting them with several heavy encyclopedias. After a few hours passed and the flowers were dry, she would lift the books and paper towels to reveal perfectly preserved pressed flowers. She then guided her grandchildren in laying the flowers on strips of cut cardboard and sealing them with clear adhesive paper. "Bookmarks," she announced, helping them tie ribbons on one end. These bookmarks were cherished throughout the school year and for many years beyond. The "flower from Granny's garden" became a prized possession for each. They proudly displayed the bookmarks that they had chosen the flowers for and helped to make. And for the rest of their lives, every time they passed a bed of pansies, they thought of Granny and her garden.

Nature is already there, waiting for us to notice it. Just as we are inherently creative beings, nature is creativity itself. It is a constant reminder of our own true nature. I like to say that the Great Creator didn't feel a need to stop, with thousands of colors, shapes, and sizes of flowers and butterflies, of snowflakes and tree leaves. Always available, nature can inspire our own growth and rebirth.

When Domenica was a toddler, she fell in love with gerbera daisies, crisp and brightly colored. We would go together to a plant store, where I would gravitate toward stargazer lilies, and Domenica would tug at my sleeve, saying, "Look, Mommy!"

pointing to the gerbera daisies. It would take only one daisy to brighten up Domenica's bedside table. My lilies were more expensive. I would ordinarily buy three stems. On days when the winter night closed in early, we would go to the plant store just as people were getting off work. I would urge Domenica to smell the lilies, warning her to be careful because their orange dust would stick to her nose. The daisies had no powdery dust, but they lacked the lilies' fragrant scent. For twelve dollars, we took home both flowers. I would stop at the Korean grocer's and buy two seven-day candles, one to place near the lilies and one to place near Domenica's daisy.

"We're building an altar," I would explain to Domenica. "Fresh flowers are important. So are candles. You might want to add a seashell and a small wooden incense holder. Now, let me make a list: what do I wish for?" Sometimes I would ask for a quality: God, grant me creativity. Grant me joy. Grant me sobriety. Grant me serenity. Domenica would copycat my prayers, although she didn't know what some of the words meant. It tickled me to hear her asking for sobriety. At six years old, she was quite sober, and, God willing, would remain that way.

When Domenica was older and had an allowance, she would pester me to go to the plant store. Her favorite gerberas were bright pink, with orange a close second. "Let's make an altar, Mommy," she would say. And so I would buy a candle from the Korean grocer on our way home. Flowers spoke to Domenica of safety and joy. When there were no lilies, she would buy me tulips, spending her entire allowance on the luxury of flowers. Today, Domenica still buys flowers. This past Mother's Day, a giant bouquet of stargazer lilies arrived on my doorstep, a nod back to the trips to the Korean grocer on that Greenwich Village corner where I shared with Domenica my own love of flowers.

Pam and Rick took their four children from suburban Milwaukee to the north woods of Wisconsin once a year, where they rented a small cottage on a lake for a week. "It was tiny," Rick says, and laughs. "But it was affordable for a large family, and it was a great adventure for the kids. We'd fish and grill and hike and swim. It was simple, but the connection to nature was something we all looked forward to." Their kids still talk about the "cabin up north" and the way they all looked forward to going. "All the kids slept up in the loft," says their son Jesse. "There was a TV with one channel, and somehow that was more exciting than the TV at home with a million channels. There was more mystery up north. We'd have to watch whatever the TV had to offer us. I think about those vacations a lot. In hindsight, they were very simple. But they felt like the greatest adventure. Going to Disneyland was amazing, but staying in that cabin in the woods was somehow even more memorable."

Noah, who grew up in northern Maine, remembers exploring in the wooded area behind his parents' house. "It was the middle of nowhere, where we were," he remembers. "Just woods, really. We lived in such a rural location, so far from civilization, that you had to drive to get anywhere. And it wasn't a short drive, either." Noah remembers his childhood fondly. "There was plenty of room for imagination in those woods," he says. "A story in every tree, really." Undistracted by the built environment of a city or suburban life, Noah's imagination was free to grow. "I was bored sometimes, but not usually," he muses. "There definitely wasn't a mall to go to, or a pool or a miniature golf course. It was a very quiet place. But I know it made me richer. When I was younger, reading the Grimms' fairy tales with my dad, I was convinced that all of the stories happened in the woods behind our house—and who's to say they didn't? It was a sort of enchanted forest." Today, Noah is a movie director who lives in Hollywood. Is it really any surprise that his work, which inhabits the family genre, consistently speaks of magic and fantasy? "There are a lot of trees in California, and I chose a lush area to live in. But I still go to Maine every chance I get. It feeds me."

It may feel like we are not giving our children "enough" by "only" going to the park. Sitting on a bench and taking a moment to quickly check our e-mail from our phone, to regroup and assess our constantly growing list of things we must accomplish, we may feel that our child, who wanders along a path nearby, would be better off in swimming lessons or art class or practicing the violin. All of these things are good, but we needn't fill every minute with structured activity. Letting our children take in the details of a flower, or gaze up at a tree where a nest of birds tells a secret story, we allow them to make their own connections and imagine what only they can conjure. Who knows? Maybe a movie is being made as we wait on our bench, scribbling our grocery list and planning tomorrow's carpool schedule. And maybe, letting ourselves have a few minutes to notice the designs in the clouds, we give ourselves a dose of optimism to share with our children as well.

ENTERING THE GARDEN
An Exercise

List five places you could take your child where he or she could be exposed to flora. Whether it is the backyard, a nearby park, or the flower section in the grocery store doesn't matter. What matters is letting your child have enough time to absorb the scents, colors, and shapes.

Examples:

I could drive my child to a farm or a community
 garden.
I could go to the library and borrow a book on flowers,
 and my child and I could choose our favorites,
 learning their names and characteristics. We could
 then find those flowers in nature or a shop, and see in
 person the flowers we feel we already know.

I could _____.
I could _____.
I could _____.
I could _____.
I could _____.

Now list five botanical adventures you could have inside the house. They should be simple and inexpensive. Bringing flora into your home can raise your spirits just as much as it enriches your child's senses.

Examples:

I could press flowers between large books, the way
  Mary did.
I could let my child choose a few flowers from the
  florist, and when we come home we could arrange
  them in a vase together, placing it somewhere
  prominent when we are done.
I could purchase a small window box or herb garden and
  plant the seeds with my child.

I could _____.
I could _____.
I could _____.
I could _____.
I could _____.

FAUNA

Few things are more enjoyable than a pet. Few things also teach
more responsibility. A pet thrives on a regular routine. Our children thrive, caring for their pets. Choosing a pet requires all of our
discernment. Young children need a child-friendly pet. There are
breeds of dog that have been bred through decades to be patient
and friendly with rambunctious youngsters. Golden retrievers and
Labradors are two such breeds. An animal must be huggable for a
toddler, and the parent must be prepared to teach "gentle" to their
child. There are also many ways of interacting with animals if the
leap of bringing a pet into the house is too great. When we were
living in New York, I would take Domenica to visit horses in

Central Park. You might visit a farm or a zoo. Tiny baby steps are large enough. A fish tank may feel like too large an endeavor, but a hummingbird feeder outside the window might bring hours of watching joy.

When Domenica was four, I got her her first dog: a snow-white standard poodle that we named Calla Lily. We selected Calla Lily out of the litter of pups because she approached Domenica rather than waiting for Domenica to approach her. She proved to be patient and loving. Domenica would cuddle with her, crooning, "Good doggie, good doggie." Before long, Calla Lily knew our routine. She would walk with me to take Domenica to school and walk with me again to pick her up. Domenica quickly learned to lead Calla Lily beside her. Calla Lily was sweet-tempered and gentle. She did not tug. We kept her trimmed in a fluffy puppy cut rather than any of the more exotic poodle cuts. Snowy white and fluffy, she resembled a lamb. Domenica would hug and kiss her, which Calla Lily not only endured but enjoyed.

When Calla Lily was a year old, we acquired a cat. Also snowy white and fluffy, the cat was named Polar Bear, and he was not available for cuddling. Instead, he remained aloof, and Domenica learned to respect his wishes. We fed our animals at opposite ends of the house. Calla Lily was not above a cat-food snack. Polar Bear would eat dog food if allowed the chance. Domenica and I made a careful ritual out of feeding each animal. When it was time for Polar Bear's dinner, he would announce his hunger with a loud "meow" as he twined himself around our legs. Cally, as we called her, learned to wait her turn.

Eric takes four-year-old Evan to the park every day, where they feed the ducks in the pond. The ducks are used to their visitors, and they quack loudly as they float toward their friends, who promise delicious bread from the shore. Evan delights in the ducks' antics, and Eric and Evan have taken to naming the ducks. "There's Sam," Evan says, and points. "There's Leo!" The ducks seem to respond to their names as they paddle toward them, accepting the food that is offered. "I let him believe that the ducks are responding to their names as well as the food," says Eric. "And who's to be sure they're not? I can't prove that they don't know their names."

Reaching out to animals and forming relationships with them builds empathy and gives all of us a deeper understanding of our own nature. Animals mirror us back to ourselves. "We're all creatures," says Eric. "It's good to remember that." Visiting the zoo, staring into the face of a baby tiger, we make a connection. Connecting to God's creatures, we remember that we are one of God's creatures, too.

If and when the time does come to bring a pet into the home, it can be a great experience of growth for a child. No longer is the child the one being taken care of. The child now must step up to the plate and care for another. It is fine to start small—a goldfish, a hamster, a newt—or you can plunge right in and commit to a cat or dog. As daunting as the idea of getting a dog may seem, bringing a companion into the house can add a deep well of joy and entertainment to the home.

"My kids begged for a dog," says Peggy. "For years they begged. I resisted because I had never had a dog myself, and I didn't know how to choose one or how to train it and care for it. So the deal was that if they both got good grades for the entire school year, we'd go to a breeder the next summer and get a puppy. It was quite the motivator." Peggy not only promised the dog as an academic reward, though. The girls, with Peggy, spent the year learning about different breeds and training techniques. By the time summer came and the girls proudly presented their glowing report cards, they were quite educated in the ways of the canine.

"It was so much more fun, and so much less intimidating, to get a dog when we kind of knew what we were doing," says Peggy. "We had really trained ourselves. The girls were ready for this animal to be work—to be a job for them. And they really wanted it. We attended training classes, read books, dog-sat for friends, and the more we learned, the more they were convinced that this was what they wanted. It actually all went pretty smoothly." Cocoa, their brown Lhasa apso, is a delightful addition to their home. It is no surprise that it went smoothly—Peggy and her girls did a lot of work beforehand. And after doing this work, it was well within their grasp to train their puppy with joy and success. It was far-seeing of Peggy to require such a large amount of work of her girls in advance of getting the dog—a year of good grades is no small feat. And a dog is no small reward. Her incentive to them was wise, as it proved to her and to the girls that they were willing to work hard for the pet they wanted so much.

"I wanted them to understand that this was a long-term commitment, requiring long-term preparation and serious attention. Asking them both to work extra-hard at their grades also paid off. It became a habit. Their grades were fine before, but they are working harder and paying more attention to them now. They've both improved, and their work ethic has improved, too. It became a friendly challenge between them, too—they both had to hold up their end of the deal, or they would let the other one down as well as themselves. They deserved the reward of Cocoa. And yes—he does add a lot of sweetness to the house."

AT HOME WITH THE ANIMAL KINGDOM
An Exercise

List your five favorite animals.

1. _____

2. _____

3. _____

4. _____

5. _____

Now ask your child to name his or her five favorite animals. Find a way to interact with one of the animals, whether at a friend's house, at a zoo, or in a park. After you have done this, ask your child to draw or write about his or her experience with the animal.

WALKING

Walking connects us with nature and with a force greater than ourselves. Call it God, the Great Creator, the source, a higher power—it doesn't matter what we name it. The point is that, in walking, we find a sense of connection. Answers come to us from "nowhere." Inspiration strikes, optimism returns. I have often advised my students to walk out with a question and see if they return with an answer. And very often, they do.

Walking also connects us to the person we are walking with. How many good conversations have been had on walks? I hear stories of plots being ironed out, relationships being improved, and, over and over again, real connections being made.

When we walk with our children, we connect with our children.

Whether our children are in strollers or walking beside us doesn't matter. Taking in the sights and sounds, country or city, we are sharing an experience of connecting to something greater than ourselves.

"Recently my eleven-year-old got really mad at me," says Laura. "I wouldn't let her see a movie that she really wanted to see. We live in a big city, and a lot of her friends are seeing it. But I think she's too young. It's dark, and I think it's rated PG-13 for a reason. She's not thirteen, and I told her she needed to wait. But she was furious. She told me that she would be the only one who hadn't seen it, and that she'd hear all about it anyway. Living in a big city, kids are exposed to too much too soon, I think. So I enforce limits where I can. I have to—or she'll think the world is just a free-for-all with so much available to her. Shortly after we had this fight, we needed to walk to school. I always drop her off on my way to work. Walking ten feet ahead of me down the city blocks, she refused to speak to me, and the only connection was her occasionally turning around to toss me a scowling glare. But I noticed something. Even though we were outside and not alone, we were, in a way, completely connected. Instead of being at home, where she could run into her room and close the door, absorbing herself in her computer or texting her friends about her evil mother, we were together. Just the two of us. The walk down the street showed our dynamic to the world—and we both had to look at it. We couldn't separate and fume on our own, reaching out to our own networks to be validated. No, we were there together, facing the feelings head-on that we both might rather avoid."

By the end of the walk, Laura and her daughter were walking a little bit closer to each other. And when Laura left her daughter at school, handing her her lunch and wishing her a good day, a tiny bit of normalcy was restored. By the end of the day, when Laura met her child to walk her home, her daughter confessed that she was not the only one forbidden to see the movie.

Because Laura and her daughter got out of the house and walked—albeit because they had to get to school—their conflict was resolved a little more quickly.

David spoke of his own experience. "My brother, sadly, is an alcoholic," David shared. "We've all tried to help him, but he goes up and down, and it's impossible to predict where his mood or behavior will be from one day to the next. His son, Josh, is ten, and it's clear that Josh isn't really right. He isolates himself, he has a temper, and he alternately lashes out and retreats into submission. The only thing I know that I can do is to be a steady presence in Josh's life. With Josh, I don't expect anything back. For me, it's about giving to him no matter what. I'll take him to a game or to the park or a movie. I'll buy him popcorn and take him home afterward. I don't force him to do anything. I just want to give him a break."

I felt for David, and encouraged him to continue reaching out to Josh. The other day, David called me, elated.

"I decided I'd try taking Josh hiking. It was a bit ambitious, but he's athletic, and I figured we could always turn back. But I had a feeling that the exercise would be great for him. He's got a lot of emotions he needs to burn off."

What David didn't see coming was that by going on a hike just with Josh, he was inviting in the magic of walking.

"We hiked for about an hour, taking breaks along the way, in almost total silence. I'd point out different kinds of trees or offer Josh some water, but he said almost nothing to me. And then, out of the blue, he just started talking. I don't know if it was because I had him captive and was willing to wait for him to initiate, or what it was. But all of a sudden, he turned to me and said, 'My dad would never go on a hike like this.' I was pretty shocked, but God knows I've been waiting for this moment. I opened up to him a little bit—I mean, his dad is my brother. And Josh is right—he wouldn't go on a hike like this now. But once upon a time, he would have. We talked about his dad. I told him some stories from when we were kids, and I let Josh know that I felt really sorry that his dad was having so much trouble right now, and that I knew that it must be hard for Josh. By the time we reached the top of the mountain and surveyed our progress, we were talking about other things. Josh was even laughing with me as I told him stories of hikes I had been on where I got caught in the rain or lost the trail. I tell you, I would have walked for days in silence to get to this moment. Now Josh and I go for a hike every weekend. We both look forward to it. It's a really simple thing, but it's important."

When David speaks of the healing power of his "captive" walks with Josh, I am filled with wonder again, even though I have observed this many times before. And being filled with wonder, again and again, is, to me, the proof that God is there with us. I do believe that when we walk, God will join us. The Great Creator is always ready and waiting for us to go on a walk—it's up to us to accept the offer.

Every Monday, when my daughter was small, we walked twenty blocks along Manhattan's Madison Avenue. It was rich window shopping, and we divided what we saw into three categories: "yes," "no," and "maybe." Taking my daughter by the hand, I would lead her from window to window, encouraging her to articulate her choices. A window full of antiques led her to exclaim "Yes!" as she spotted a paperweight with a tiger lily encased in glass. Another window invited "No," as she saw nothing that captured her fancy.

"Yes," I would say, viewing a window filled with designer frocks.

"Maybe," she would say, less enchanted with them than I. Although I didn't think of it in these terms at the time, I was educating my daughter's eye. As she grew older, her "yes," "no," and "maybe" grew more decisive. There were objects she clearly loved, and other objects that left her indifferent. A window that held a painting of an English Thoroughbred horse received and excited "yes." A window full of Chinese vases ranked another "yes."

In cold weather and in warm, we walked our beat. The fresh air was tonic. The walk was invigorating. Settling on the day's choices was exciting.

It is now twenty-five years later, and my grown daughter still enjoys walking and window-shopping.

TO OUR DESTINATION

An Exercise

Take a walk with your child with a special destination in mind. It may be a street where you like to window-shop or a favorite café. It may be a nearby park. Whatever it is, allow yourselves to anticipate the adventure and be conscious of taking in the sights and sounds together as you walk. Notice if your conversation starts to fall naturally in step with the physical rhythm of your gait.

GRATITUDE

For many of us, counting our blessings is a new procedure. We go through life unconscious. We do not count the many good things that we experience, but we can easily name each negative experience in painful detail. Optimism is an elected attitude and it is the reward for counting our blessings. When we make a point of enumerating the many good things we enjoy, our list of blessings grows ever longer. At first we may name only a few blessings, but as we name them, they seem to multiply.

"I am grateful for my healthy children" becomes "I am grateful for their good energy" becomes "I am grateful for their good humor." As we list our blessings and the benefits they convey, we find ourselves happier and more secure. As we count the ways in which God has blessed us, we look to God for further blessings.

Naming the gifts we have received, we find ourselves noting even more. Gratitude breeds gratitude.

"It's so easy to go through the world just stressed," admitted Babs, a mother of six, when I spoke with her one morning. "I mean, the number of times I've told the person working in the grocery store that she's not moving fast enough. Or said to a perfect stranger, 'I'll talk to you when you have six kids.' The other day I actually told someone he was talking too slowly. I asked him for directions, he started to give them to me, and I cut him off before he was done, sure I'd figure it out more quickly myself. I mean, who do I think I am?" Babs laughed at herself in retrospect. A larger-than-life, loud, and colorful personality, Babs runs a happy and hectic household with a great deal of success. I pointed this out to her, urging her to try writing a gratitude list, even if it felt like a colossal waste of time.

"I mean, if anyone but you suggested I try this, God knows what I'd say," said Babs. "But okay. I'll try it."

Babs reported back to me in five minutes.

"First of all, it took five minutes," she confessed to me. "I dismissed it, thinking I don't have time for these little games. I thought it would take me all day and take me away from what really had to be done. But guess what? I am going to be a nicer person today because I did it."

Babs read me her gratitude list:

Six healthy children
A supportive and hilarious husband who has a great job
The support of my weight-loss group
That we live in California, where every day is beautiful
My sister, who lives down the street

My great hair—I don't have to spend any time styling it
The bulk food store near the house
The schools in our district
The local children's theater
Our church community

As I listened to Babs's list, I was struck by how blessed her life is. It was impossible to miss the large and many gifts she had to be grateful for on a daily basis.

"I'm so happy I did this," said Babs. "I can already tell you I'm going to be more patient with everyone I cross paths with today. And I also feel more patient with myself."

It can be understandably frustrating for a busy parent like Babs to be told to "relax and find time for herself." We may think that we need a vacation, a nanny, a long stretch of completely empty time—in other words, whatever it is we cannot have. But it's not so much about finding vast swaths of empty time. It's more about finding time to pay attention—in Babs's case, just five minutes. When she pays attention to how she is doing, and pays attention to everything that is already right in her life, it brings her a sense of peace and relief.

I told Babs I'd give her a quick call at the end of the day to see how the rest of her day played out after trying this exercise.

"Oh, there were plenty of dramas and frantic moments. But I can tell you that I didn't raise my voice once more today," she tells me when we check in again that evening. "I'm trained as an opera singer, and believe me, my voice carries," she says, chuckling.

"Did you feel like you had a little bit of a calmer day after starting it off with gratitude?" I ask.

"I do," she muses. "And during dinner, I was watching my

husband helping the kids and telling jokes. I remembered putting him on my gratitude list that morning. He is hilarious and supportive. He does have a good job that allows us to have a comfortable life. He caught me staring at him at one point, and I just winked at him. I'm not going to tell him he was on my list. But I felt us connect in that moment. I know he can feel my gratitude for him, and I know I can choose to show it to him, too."

The gratitude list is a shockingly powerful tool. So often it feels like "everything" is wrong, when that is never the case. Listing our blessings can startle us into gratitude by reminding us of the many things that are right in our lives. This tool does not need to take more than a few minutes, and can be fun for our children to try, as well. It can even be simplified to listing things they "like" in their lives. The spiritual shift in perspective is the same.

GRATEFUL FOR GRATITUDE
An Exercise

Both you and your child will benefit from expressing gratitude. Together, take turns naming one thing you are grateful for. Gratitude relieves pressure, and this exercise will naturally restore an emotional balance.

Choose one item that you named and ask your child to do the same. Now make a "creative offering" referencing the thing you are grateful for—draw a picture of it, write a song about it, make up a poem. As you and your child share your offerings with each other, you cherish and honor that which you are grateful for.

Chapter Four

CULTIVATING LIMITS

~

In limits, there is freedom. Creativity thrives within structure. Although we may picture true creativity as being a sort of "free for all," the opposite is actually true. When we set boundaries, our children feel loved. The paradox of creative expansion is that the greatest freedom lies within safe boundaries. This applies to physical space as well. Creating safe havens where our children are allowed to dream, play, make a mess, and, yes, clean it up, we teach them respect for themselves and others, and the joy of a warm and enticing physical and spiritual environment.

STRUCTURE

Sometimes, in our desire to raise accomplished children, we over-book and overschedule their young lives. What is ideal is a structured mixture of scheduled and unscheduled time. Giving their day a thoughtful framework, we can provide balance and variety. Incorporating scheduled and unscheduled time into a firmly structured day, our children are given enough guidance as well as ample breaks and rest. Achieving this happy medium, we can be flexible as well. And although it is important to provide structure, it is also important to allow for spontaneity.

Returning from school, my daughter Domenica seemed to do best when I would greet her with open arms and snacks, and allow her an hour to simply unwind. We can offer our children a choice of activities—perhaps a game of checkers or some free time in the backyard. We can also offer them our time and attention, asking, "How was your day?" and listening attentively as they respond. Domenica rode a stick horse to school, and I would meet her at day's end with the same stick horse for her to ride home. We lived in New York, in Greenwich Village, and there was an excellent pizza stand adjacent to the school.

"Pizza?" I would ask her, and she often said yes. So we would ride the stick horse to the pizza stand and hobble it to a table while we devoured our pizza and debriefed on our day. It was a short ten-minute walk back to our loft, and once we were there, I would offer Domenica a choice of activities. Most days, she opted for playing with her Breyer horses, although some days her dolls won out. I noticed that she had a predilection for alone time. She didn't want Mommy—she wanted play. I would give her that hour to play freely, and then we would turn our focus to her homework. I would try to lighten her learning with gentle, fun nudges, often making a game out of guessing the correct answers. After a decompressing hour of play, Domenica came to her homework refreshed and willing to work. Her happily anticipated hour of playtime was within the greater structure of a predictable routine, which gave her a feeling of security.

Every creative endeavor thrives in an environment of safety. One of the quickest ways to create this environment is to provide structure. As parents, we seek a balance: the greatest freedom lies within structure, but if we overschedule, we leave no room for spontaneity or inspiration.

We live in a time when opportunity floods us and our children, and it would be quite possible to fill every moment of every day with yet another educational or enlightening activity. In an effort to educate and sophisticate our children, we can push them past the point of childlike discovery and into resentment.

Christine Koh, lifestyle and parenting blogger and author of *Minimalist Parenting*, puts it this way: "I see our kids' lives get overscheduled all the time. There's so much available to us and our children that it's possible to overdo practically everything. And we have to be careful—it's the parent's responsibility to give our kids room to make their own decisions. If we keep feeding them the next activity, we are not helping them develop as independent thinkers. We are teaching them that someone else will always tell them what comes next."

If children are not given the freedom to make creative decisions on their own—including decisions about how they will spend their time—they will at first rebel, and soon thereafter become habituated to finding their answers and ideas in outside sources. There is little that can dampen their creative development more than taking away their freedom of choice and experimentation.

And so we must strike a gentle balance within which our children can learn and rest. Ian, a seven-year-old aspiring drummer, has a drumming lesson that dictates his schedule for much of his week. On Thursdays, he looks forward to the drive to the studio, where he will spend an hour with his teacher, showing him the fruits of his practicing from the week before, and be given assignments for the week to come. In between lessons, he practices thirty minutes a day or more. "I make sure it's at least thirty minutes," says his mother, Elizabeth. "That's the rule. But sometimes he goes longer." The trick is to set a goal that is low enough to meet regularly. Thirty minutes is possible for Ian to accomplish on a daily basis. It's small enough that he feels empowered to achieve it, but large enough that he makes significant progress. If he goes beyond thirty minutes of practice, wonderful. If he becomes inspired and doesn't want to stop, there is no reason to stop him. Elizabeth is careful to leave enough room in Ian's schedule that he can indeed practice his drums longer than the required thirty minutes if he is so inclined. By giving him room for his passion to grow, she allows his enthusiasm to take over. Enthusiastic, he wants to work at his craft. In so doing, his skills build with speed and joy.

Within the framework of a gentle discipline, enthusiasm grows on its own, builds on itself. Elizabeth knows that half an hour a day of practice will develop the skills necessary for Ian to actually enjoy playing. As he gains momentum, his drum practice falls easily within the expectations of a "disciplined" schedule, but, because his practice is also motivated by inspiration from within, he is more likely to maintain the excitement and passion that will give his art longevity.

Structure provides a prepared environment for inspiration. Scheduling our children so that they are exposed to a variety of activities, while being cautious to leave room for their interests to grow, we give them the gift of safety and an environment in which their creativity can develop along their own authentic callings.

NAMING TALENTS
An Exercise

Despite our best intentions of exposing our children to art and values that we care about, we cannot control where their interests or talents will lie. We must simply grant them the tools and empower them to pursue their enthusiasms.

List five talents you see in yourself.

1. _____
_____
2. _____
_____
3. _____
_____
4. _____
_____
5. _____
_____

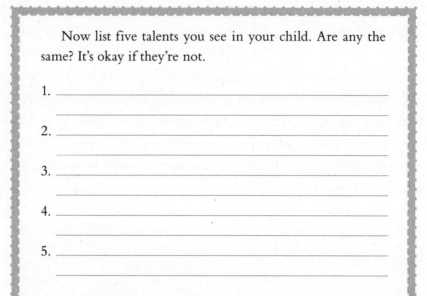

Now list five talents you see in your child. Are any the same? It's okay if they're not.

1. _____
   _____

2. _____
   _____

3. _____
   _____

4. _____
   _____

5. _____
   _____

By honestly assessing each of your positive traits, you see where you are alike and where you are different. Seeing ourselves and one another with accuracy and honesty, we become closer, appreciating and acknowledging our individuality. Appreciating our children's individuality, we are guided to structure their days along the lines of their true values as well.

A PLACE FOR EVERYTHING

We don't always have all the room that we wish for, but we can start by husbanding the space that we do have. Clutter is distracting and discouraging for us as well as for our children, so decluttering is a great first step.

If we can designate a place for everything—"everything in its place," as my mother, Dorothy, always said—we are in a very good place indeed. But before doing this, we must rid ourselves of that which is unnecessary, unneeded, or unwanted.

If your home is not already organized—and most people fall into this category—there are many small, simple ways to start to declutter and make space for what you really want in your life and in your child's life. One of my favorite tools is to set a timer for fifteen minutes, and in that time, throw away, give away, or put away as much as possible. Children love to be involved in this game. The timer makes it fun (for us, too, I may add!) and sets a reasonable, accomplishable goal with immediate and gratifying results.

"Three . . . two . . . one . . . go!" and everyone starts racing around the house. I like to designate empty boxes as "give away" and "throw away" boxes. Perhaps there is a prize for the child who rids himself or herself of the most in the fifteen minutes. Maybe the child gets to choose an ice cream flavor at the grocery store or decide on the television show that will be watched during family time. If toys and belongings have a place of their own, it's easy—simply return each item to its designated place. If something is determined to be trash, toss it into the "throw away" box. (You can check to be sure that the items in this box are indeed trash at the end of the session!) Setting up a box for recycling also reinforces the separation of trash and recyclables for our children. In the boxed marked "give away," toss all items that are not trash in and of themselves, but that are only adding clutter to your home and would do better in a new home.

Charlotte recalls these fifteen-minute cleanup sessions with fondness. "My dad and I would run circles in my room, because now we could," she says with a laugh. "I chronically threw things on the floor. But learning that I really could make an impact in fifteen minutes helped me a lot. I still use the tool—I call it 'doing a fifteen.'" Charlotte remembers the feeling of elation when she could see the floor of her room again. "The truth is, I love having a clean, neat house," she says. "It's like a whole different world."

Indeed. When we clear the physical space, we literally make room for clarity and inspiration. Respecting our space, we respect ourselves. Our space is where we live, where we reflect, where we have ideas and find a sense of grounded safety. As long as that space is open—literally—we are open to a flow of good, and a flow of good ideas.

As much as our children may love to strew their toys all over the living room floor and jump on their beds until pillows fly everywhere, I have yet to meet a child who doesn't actually function better when that mess is restored to some semblance of serenity. What is more enticing to jump on, anyway, than a bed arranged with fluffy pillows? In giving our children order, we give them safety. In giving them safety, we give them the space to take creative flight.

Virtually every parent I have known, observed, and spoken to in the process of writing this book has mentioned the physical clutter that amasses and the struggle to keep up with it. I urge parents not to fret about it too much: although decluttering seems like an unattainable goal, it is not impossible. Even just fifteen minutes a day, over the long run, makes a huge impact. Involving our children makes an even greater one. It is empowering to discard that which we no longer need, and our children learn this quickly. And as the special, ratty toy is saved, the few cherished items gain more value as they are chosen from the rubble and given a special place of honor. It is a paradox that the less we hold on to, the more we have. Throwing away that which is old and broken leaves room for the exciting toy that was overlooked and forgotten. Rather than a mess of weathered items, we save a few valuable ones and have a collection of chosen toys and objects that carry true meaning.

"Doing a fifteen" is worthwhile even when the house appears to be clean and picked up. Taking fifteen minutes in a junk drawer or a closet also reveals treasures and trash, and always, always opens the door to optimism. I have watched many parents lament over a house that was "too small" until they cleared clutter, often finding that their house was "big enough" after all.

Clearing clutter clears our psyche as much as it clears our physical space. Tripping over the same toy several times in a day, our nerves become raw and our skin becomes thin. But small steps toward order can have a large impact on our environment and our children's, spiritually, mentally, and physically.

Once we have established a place for everything, making a mess is less threatening. Toys may be scattered in the living room, provided that when they are done being played with, they are safely stored away. My childhood playroom, with its several large trunks, was ready for order to be restored. In Domenica's playroom, I copycatted my mother's use of trunks. There was one for toy horses, one for blocks, and one for dolls and doll clothes. Domenica knew which trunk was which, and the simple sorting of her toys taught her the value of order.

"But Julia! I have so much clutter. You can't imagine how

much. I could never get rid of it!" I know. It feels like a mountain that is unscalable, like a truly impossible feat. Clutter blocks our flow. It muddies our water and adds stress to our day. But taking our clutter one piece at a time, it is possible, quite possible, to become clutter-free in less time than we are afraid it might take. The trick is to take it in bite-sized increments. Fifteen minutes at a time, we can make an impact. Clearing clutter always allows us to start anew.

THE SEVENTY-TWO PICKUP
An Exercise

Growing up, when the mess got out of hand, it was time for a game my mother called "Seventy-two Pickup." It consists of the children putting the toys away in seventy-two seconds while the adult counts out the tempo. With seven Cameron children, there was seven times the mess—and seven times the frenzy as we threw toys and art supplies into their designated trunks.

Take a cue from Dorothy Cameron and try the "Seventy-two Pickup" game with your child. This works regardless of how many children or how many toys you are dealing with. Count backward from seventy-two to zero and allow yourself and your children a sense of play and accomplishment in this race against the (human) clock.

A ROOM OF THEIR OWN

Although Virginia Woolf suggested that all artists need a room of their own, not all of us have the extra space to achieve this. But it is worth pursuing, for ourselves and our children, and we can create these special areas, however small they might be, inspired by safety, magic, and ideas.

As we clear clutter, we find that we have more room, physically and psychically. And just as we need to have room enough for our creative endeavors, our children need to have space of their own. It is important to designate an area that is strictly our children's. Teresa, a young mother in England, exposed her daughter to the Flower Fairy books at a young age. Together they would pore over the pictures, reading the stories and making up their own. In the garden, they would point out the different flowers and muse over which Flower Fairy existed magically within each one. When the family moved to Germany, much was new for Teresa's daughter. They could bring only their most valuable possessions with them, and they chose the cherished items carefully when they packed up their things. When they got to their new home, Teresa watched as her daughter carted her Flower Fairy book everywhere with her, clutching it tightly on car trips and turning its pages as she sat in the corner of their new living room, where everything—including the language spoken around them—had changed.

Teresa was suddenly struck with an idea: there was a cubbyhole in a large walk-in closet in their new house. What if she were to make it a special place for her daughter? Remembering how much she had loved the secret compartments built into the walls of the house she had grown up in herself, she wallpapered the cubbyhole with Flower Fairy wallpaper, added a small chair and a Flower Fairy lamp, and hung a Flower Fairy curtain as a doorway that could be closed if her daughter wanted privacy in her secret space.

Her daughter, now grown, still remembers the thrill of having a room of her own. "Turning on the lamp and seeing the fairies illuminated, I felt like it was all real. It was a magical place where Flower Fairies lived. I would read my book or sit there with my stuffed animals or my cat. The little room was rich with possibility and fantasy. To this day I have wonderfully fond memories of those books, and cozy spaces always speak to me." Giving our children the gift of space, and adding even the simplest touches that make that space truly theirs, we give our children room to imagine, to dream, and to become themselves.

Creating space that is habitable and inviting helps everyone, and we can look for areas of our homes that might be improved for our own benefit as well. And when we take care of ourselves in this way, the happy by-product is that it also helps our children.

"For almost a year, my terrace has been basically unusable," says Jenn, calling long-distance from Miami. It is the first I have heard of her having a terrace. I tell her as much. "I know," Jenn laments. "We have a grill out there, which is great. And my husband uses that. But there's a huge table filling up practically the whole space—it gets crowded as soon as two people are out there— and the tiles, chairs, and table are filthy. It's basically a kind of dirty storage unit in view of the street."

I ask Jenn what she thinks it would take to bring it to a more usable condition. "Well, probably just a bucket of hot, soapy water, a sponge, and a little elbow grease," she admits. "We need a smaller table, but the huge one folds in half and could be stored off to the side."

I let her know that the project, in fact, doesn't sound very large. "What would happen if you spent fifteen minutes on this?" I ask her.

"I'll try it," Jenn says. "I didn't have any plans for the next fifteen minutes, anyway," she laughs. "What was I going to do? Check my e-mail? Browse the Internet? I'm turning on the hot water and getting the bucket out now. I'll call you back in fifteen."

I smile to myself as I hang up the phone, knowing full well that the progress she will make in that window will astonish and relieve her.

In twelve-step jargon, there is talk of "progress, not perfection." This is a good mantra for us as well, as we guide our creative children and attend to the creative children in ourselves. A little goes a long way. That means a little praise, a little encouragement, a little down-on-hands-and-knees scrubbing. It is far harder and more painful to be a blocked artist than it is to do the work. It is far harder and more painful to try to look the other way every time we pass the terrace window, wincing and feeling discouraged, than it is to fill the bucket with water and clean it up. Incremental progress adds up much faster than we would assume. The pain of not taking this small step is far more destructive to our psyche and productivity than just being willing to take a few minutes and toss a few things out or make a space habitable. One thing leads to the next, and letting go of the unwanted makes way for the new and surprising.

My phone rings again, and it is Jenn.

"First of all, it's hotter than blazes out there," she tells me. I already hear the levity in her voice.

"Well, good. You're well into grilling season, then. Perfect timing," I reply.

"And I have to tell you that that scrubbing is a bit of a workout," Jenn goes on.

"Good!" I say. "You like to work out." To say that she is a fitness enthusiast is a vast understatement. There is hardly a day when she doesn't surf, swim, or lift weights.

Jenn laughs. "Fair enough. But here's the thing: I started scrubbing, and it was really, really dirty out there. The tiles were literally black. But I realized a few things."

"Let's hear them."

"First of all, if you had asked me what color my tiles were, I would have told you gray. They're white," she says, chuckling. "Second, fifteen minutes is significant. You can get a lot done. I even want to do another fifteen minutes when I hang up. Because I realized that I have a terrace. I'm lucky. It's beautiful. I have an ocean view, and I had literally shoved a bunch of clutter between me and the reason I bought this apartment."

I listen, feeling for her.

"And now," she continues, "I know exactly what to do with my short story that I was stuck on. I'm going to finish cleaning the terrace, set my daughter up with her drawing pad next to me, and sit out there with my laptop, with an unobstructed view of the Atlantic, and write. Each tile I scrub helps sort out my story line. And my daughter keeps yelling, 'Water! Water!' I've been blocking the view from her, too."

I'm thrilled to hear her clarity and excitement, and not surprised. Over and over, my students have reported not only physical but also creative breakthroughs they have had almost immediately upon clearing clutter and husbanding their space.

Using the space we have, we literally make room for our ideas. Creating a room of our own, however small, we are inspired to take action in larger ways as well.

A ROOM OF YOUR OWN
An Exercise

Taking a cue from Teresa and Jenn, look around your home and see if there is a place that could become a sort of "creative haven" for you or your child. Ideally, you can create one for each of you. Allow the space to be small, if square feet are an issue. It is the quality, vibrancy, and thoughtfulness of the space that matters more than the size of the space itself.

MISUNDERSTANDING MESSINESS

Children love mess, and it is important that we allow them to create chaos. The child who is overcontrolled is a child who misses the glee of play. Artists of any age love play. Play is messy. For all of us, the part of us that creates is our own "inner child." We may be tired of hearing about the "inner child," but as we observe our children and reflect on ourselves, we recognize the part of ourselves that is also youthful, playful, and uninhibited by outer limits or rules. Giving our inner artist—as well as our child—room to be messy is freeing and enlivening for all.

Angie's California home is sleek and bright, a modern house with clean lines and new amenities. She bought it recently with her young family, and upon moving in, she realized she was trying to "preserve the perfection" in a way that was frustrating herself, her husband, and her young son, Richard.

"I loved the shininess of it when we moved in," says Angie. "I've never lived in such a new place or had such modern appliances. I wanted to keep it just like new." But with three-year-old Richard and a busy lifestyle, this was not a realistic possibility. A quest to maintain perfection is actually a blocking technique: because we can never, ever be perfect, the obsession with chasing perfection can effectively block other, more creative ideas that wish to bubble to the surface. Striving for perfection, while it may sound noble, is actually a cleverly disguised technique for closing the door on our creativity and, by extension, that of our child.

Angie quickly saw that she was not going to be able to maintain perfect order in her home, and, even if she could, it would not be the most joyous use of her time. "At first I was cleaning up after everyone all the time. I resented my son for scattering toys everywhere, and I resented my husband for leaving a wet towel in the bedroom or a dish in the sink. Before I knew it, I was a martyred wife. I never thought I even had that side of myself." Angie's story is a common one. Rather than listen to the inklings of creative desires in herself, she focused on the handprint on the refrigerator or the crooked book on the bookshelf. Entire days would pass when she had done nothing but clean up. On those days, she fell into bed exhausted and unsatisfied. "I felt like I wasn't doing anything with myself," she complained. And in fact, she was right.

When we fall into the trap of spending our days attempting to correct all superficial imperfections—be they imperfections in our surroundings or in our bodies—we are indeed "not doing anything with ourselves." Because we are all creative, we all have daily creative urges, large and small, that, left untended, will fester into sadness and resentment. I urged Angie to try a simple exercise.

"Fill in the blank five times," I told her. "If it weren't too messy, I'd try . . ."

Annie started to fill out her list. At first, what she found didn't really surprise her. "If it weren't too messy, I'd let Richard take over the kitchen table with his finger paints. If it weren't too messy, I'd encourage my husband to do more grilling. He loves to grill." But as Angie continued, her own wishes started to emerge. "If it weren't too messy, I'd plant a new batch of flowers in the front garden. If it weren't too messy, I'd think about getting my own oil paints back out and fooling around with them again." Angie was shocked to learn that much of what was waiting to be set free was her own creativity. Planting flowers, painting—these were things that Angie had deemed less important than raising a family in a perfectly clean and ordered house. I urged Angie to experiment just a little bit with allowing herself and her family some messiness, and to get back to me with what she found.

"First of all," she reported, "Richard absolutely loved the finger-painting project. I haven't seen him so happy—or, actually, so focused—in quite a while. I couldn't believe how long he was occupied with the paints. Even more shocking was that it took only a few minutes to clean up when he was done. I was so scared of making a mess that I had become afraid to start anything. I had a completely unrealistic, fear-based expectation of what it would take to clean up. And so the next day I got his paints out again, and this time, I got my own out, too. I think we might start painting together every day."

I was thrilled to hear that Angie was indulging in something of her own alongside Richard. What could be better for Richard, I thought, than a mother modeling the creative giddiness of painting beside him? Certainly not a mother whose worry about cleanup was palpable. Our children notice what we do and feel—and that includes the unspoken worry about cleaning up the mess that is being created. Exposed to a parent who is also willing to play with paint, willing to "fool around" with colors and shapes, Richard's creativity is bound to know no limits. Richard can also learn to help clean up his things and, more important, learn that it is worth starting something even if it will make a mess. If we are unwilling to ever make a mess, we are teaching our children that we are unwilling to start projects, unwilling to try new things. As we model the excitement of play in an artistic endeavor, and the willingness to clean up without drama or resentment, we are showing our children that they, too, can experiment, and that beginning a project is something to be eagerly anticipated instead of avoided.

MAKE A MESS
An Exercise

Make a mess with your child. When you are done, time the cleanup. You may be surprised at what an impact only five minutes can make. By jumping right into the cleanup, you are showing your child—and yourself—that mess is not threatening or an imaginary creative block. It is part of a thrilling process in which you can both play freely.

RESPECT

We teach our children to say "Please" and Thank you" as we model these behaviors ourselves. If we are genuine and gracious with the bus driver, our children learn to do the same. If we are honest and generous in our communication with our spouse, our children learn that, too. Children mimic what we do and absorb it. If we set boundaries with kindness, our children learn that boundary setting is okay. If we are impatient or judgmental, our children learn to emulate that as well.

No parent is perfect, and no child has even a day of "perfect" behavior. But if we are conscious of our own basic behavior and way of operating with others, we can set a deliberate example. If there is one thing that we can be guaranteed of as parents, it is that our children are watching us. They are learning from what we do, positive, negative, or indifferent. And suddenly our behavioral choices are very important.

As we model and coach our children to have respect for and be kind to others, we teach them to behave in society in a way that will help them make friends and allies in the world. Most of us have a good sense of how to do this.

When Domenica was little, I worked hard at instilling manners. "What do we say?" I would ask her when she made a request. She soon learned "Please." "What do we say?" I would ask her when I performed some task on her behalf. She learned to say "Thank you." These simple niceties stood her in very good stead. When she would go to play at a friend's house, she took her manners with her, and I was often complimented on her amenities. Soon enough, Domenica had learned not only the correct answers but also the cues. I would overhear her playing, teaching what she had learned to her dolls and stuffed animals. Her young friends quickly picked up Domenica's "rules." "I want the dolly, *please*," I would hear them say. Domenica's teachers were often appreciative of her decorum. "Domenica has good manners," I would hear at parent-teacher meetings.

Now that Domenica is grown, her manners have grown along with her. "Please" and "Thank you" are never out of style.

We are more creative when we feel respected. My friend Max, an art teacher, says that in the classroom, respect is the only "rule" that really matters. "It's about mutual respect," he says. "Sometimes teachers try to command respect by putting students down, instilling fear or intimidating them, but I don't think that really works. My philosophy is to treat them as I'd like to be treated: with warmth, politeness, kindness, and humor. And to never ask them to do anything I wouldn't do myself."

Is it a surprise that Max is beloved among his students and has many times won the title of "Teacher of the Year"?

It's not always easy, though, to maintain this dynamic. From the outside, Max seems to have an effortless, warm control of his classroom, and I tell him as much. "Don't you ever disagree with your students?" I ask him.

"All the time. Every day. Countless times." He smiles. "But I think it's very important for them to know that we're not always going to get along." A father as well as a teacher, Max says that his home and classroom life have certain similarities. "There's a time and place for 'Because I said so,'" he tells me. "Sometimes as a teacher or parent, you do know what is right for the child, whether it feels fair to them or not. In the long run it all works out. In the moment, there's sometimes some turbulence. But it's important not to get into a negotiation in these moments. I think when we allow a child to negotiate in a way that is not respectful, we are teaching them to be manipulative people. It's important to keep an eye on that."

Basic human respect and common courtesy are lessons we must be willing to teach, and good behavior is something we must be conscious to model. Whether it is for our immediate family, an elderly neighbor, the person working at the grocery store checkout, or a close friend, a doctor, a lawyer, a painter, or a filmmaker, every person deserves our respect. Regardless of class or sociocultural norms, every person we encounter deserves our warm hello and our acts of kindness.

As we demonstrate good manners in the world and also in relation to speaking about creativity in the world, our children mimic and emulate our behavior. Demonstrating a respect for artists and creative urges, we acknowledge the creativity in ourselves and others. Treating others as we wish to be treated ourselves, our children learn to do the same. And as we—and our children— reach out to the world with warmth, the world often reaches back in kind.

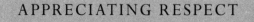

APPRECIATING RESPECT
An Exercise

List five ways you appreciate being treated. If your child is old enough, ask him or her to do this exercise as well.

Examples:

I appreciate when someone listens to me without interrupting.

I appreciate the stranger who smiles and says "Good morning" when we pass on the street.

I appreciate someone seeing the positive in what I have done.

1. _____
   _____
2. _____
   _____
3. _____
   _____
4. _____
   _____
5. _____
   _____

Now find an opportunity today to treat another person with thoughtful kindness, as you would wish to be treated yourself.

Chapter Five

CULTIVATING
SELF-EXPRESSION

Every person has a self to express, and our children feel joyful when they are able to voice their inner realities. Once we have provided safety through structure and thoughtful limits, they are ready to boldly express themselves, as are we. We provide our children with the blank canvas, and then we must step back and allow them to fill it as they will. We give them the opportunity for self-expression, and we reward them with appreciation for their acts of creativity. Documenting their creations and discoveries, we promise to remember their efforts. Our delight in their endeavors teaches them that they are in fact delightful. This knowledge gives wings to their spirit.

PROVIDING THE BLANK CANVAS

When we provide our children with the tools and materials necessary to begin a project, we give them the freedom to begin making their own creative choices. Embarking on this journey, they are empowered to make something from nothing—to fill the blank canvas.

My friends Cindi and Jeff are energetic parents to four energetic boys. Their household is joyful, and I am struck by how creatively free all four boys are, despite their wide range of personalities.

"Children just want to make the people they love proud," says Jeff. "They fear breaking the rules and coloring outside the lines, but only if others show displeasure with their choices. Rules regarding safety or respect for others make perfect sense, but arbitrary rules imposed to make adults feel comfortable may create artificial boundaries and choke off creativity." The blank canvas that is provided, literally and figuratively, by my friends leaves room for their sons to develop each of their unique gifts. "Since creation is a bit of an act of rebellion," Cindi says, laughing, "I like to encourage the inner rebel." Their light touch combined with the obvious love for their sons gives their children a wide berth in which they may navigate their way toward specificity and originality, toward true expressions of themselves.

A friend of mine is a designer whose costumes have been seen on stages and screens many times over. She has built, over the long years of her career, an impressive studio, where she creates her designs. Bright and sunny and filled with every color and texture of fabric, buttons, and trimmings, it is a magician's workshop where a sense that anything can happen seems to hang in the air. She routinely opens her doors to her nieces and nephews, allowing them to touch anything and everything.

"It's fabric," she says to me. "It's visceral. It's tactile. I tell my nieces and nephews that they can use anything they want, as long as they treat it with respect and clean up after they're done. I'll let them bring friends, and I'll help them sew." The children's awe is clear when they enter the studio. I visited her recently and watched as she happily led the children through her stashes of treasures.

"This is silk from Japan," she explained, as a young blond girl reached a chubby hand toward a bolt of shimmering dark purple and green. "Do you like this?" The girl nodded, eyes wide. She led the child to a globe situated in the corner, explaining where the silkworms had come from and pointing to the part of Japan where the fabric had been made. Cutting her a sample of the silk, she showed the girl to a table and began to discuss what they would make.

"I don't have any problem giving away my supplies," my designer friend tells me. "They can use anything here. Why not expose them to the best that there is and let them use what I am using? As long as I can instill an appreciation of the care that went into making it before it came to my studio, I am ensuring that they will go forward with an understanding of the artistry that preceded them. I believe that will inspire their own."

Setting an example of how she understands and appreciates the complete process of her creations, my friend is exposing her young relatives to the life of a working artist. Seeing her hard at work, seeing the workshop where her designs are created from drawing to mannequin, and seeing the fruits of her labors worn by actors and models when they are complete, the children are gifted with the knowledge that artistic creation requires concentrated effort and discipline, not merely inspiration. Seeing each step and coming to know the many hours their aunt spends at work, they understand that a working artist is simply another working professional. They witness the creative process firsthand as drawings are thrown out, hems are resewn, cuffs are recut. By sharing her creative kingdom and making herself a living example of the journey from vision to creation, my friend is teaching these children enormous lessons of perseverance and passion.

As we provide the blank canvas, our own joy lies in sitting back and watching what will grow from it. Handing over tools and supplies, we then observe what our children will make with them. They will always surprise us. Sophy, organizing her children's old toys for her three-year-old grandson, separated cowboy toys, monster toys, castle toys, and dinosaurs. Her grandson immediately shook things up, putting cowboys in the castle and monsters in her purse. "The one thing I know about my grandkids is that I don't know what they're thinking, ever." Sophy laughs. "All I can do is open doors and let them know I'm excited about them walking through them. If they want to play with this toy or that one, or mix things up in a way I'd never think of, then I'll certainly let them. And I'll enjoy stepping back and seeing what emerges."

As we consciously "step back and see what emerges," we open ourselves to the magic of creation—the creations our children will conjure, as well as the creation of our children's interests and passions. "Anything can lead to anywhere," Sophy muses, a twinkle in her eye. "Let's see where they go."

THE CREATIVITY CORNER
An Exercise

Create a "creativity corner" in your home where your child can go to begin projects. Stock this corner with assorted items that can provide inspiration—corks, Q-tips, toilet-paper rolls, sequins, glue, yarn, pipe cleaners, beads, tissue paper . . . As you find things in your home that may belong there, add them to the stash. If you do not have a corner free, the "creativity corner" could be a box or a shelf. The point is to designate an area where your child can find—and add to—an assortment of supplies to fill the blank canvas.

THE MAGIC OF CREATION

Children have vivid imaginations. They appreciate the magic of creation. Our job is to let them explore freely and to praise them for their efforts. The experience of making something from nothing, be it a work of art, a delicious dinner, or a page of pictures in our scrapbook, is the very definition of creativity. Creativity is a spiritual issue, and making something from nothing is a spiritual experience.

Left to their own devices, children will make something wonderful out of nothing. Free play expands the imagination. Domenica had a favorite toy horse that she "galloped" around the living room. One day, galloping was not enough. She opened the trunk containing her blocks, and she built a fence to contain her toy horse. The next day, she built a fence and a stable out of books. Now she had the makings of a story.

"It's raining," she announced, and put her toy horse into his stable.

"It's not raining," she announced, and took him back out to his corral. A few days later, Domenica added a second horse. "Friends," she announced. It took nearly all her blocks to make a stable big enough for both horses.

"It's raining," she pronounced, as she placed each horse in shelter.

"That's a good story," I told her. She was proud.

As I write this, I speak with my friend who is vacationing with his family. "I'm watching my nephew," he tells me. "We're at the pool, and he's learning how to build a sand moat from an older kid—maybe a six-year-old. My nephew's mom, my older sister, is sitting back and watching. My nephew looks like he's in heaven."

He "looks like he's in heaven," I muse. I would argue that in some way, he is. No matter our age, our level of experience or expertise, our financial status or work situation, we can all, always, create something. Taking creative action puts us in touch with a higher power—call it God, the source, inspiration, nature, or even just optimism—and once we have begun, we are partnered by something greater than ourselves.

Watching children play, I see their focus and contentment. Playing alone, they talk to themselves or to their toys. They narrate what they are doing. To whom are they speaking? Is it really "just" to themselves? Or is there something in youth that is still closer to that greater source, that accesses it more immediately? And who are we to interrupt the conversation between our children and their higher power?

Whether we define the magic of creation literally—as in Creation itself—or as something else—perhaps a sense of possibility—we are talking about the same thing. I have often said that one of our chief barriers to accepting God's generosity is our own limited notion of what we are able to accomplish. "With God as my source, all things are possible," we say. Looking more closely at this sentence, what we are saying is that God is the source of our good, the source of ideas, inspiration, and clarity. And with God as our source, we are in the spiritual position of having an unlimited bank account. It is not God who runs out of ideas, or money, or hope. It is we who turn away, deciding that there is no more for us. This behavior—and it is a learned behavior, I might add—is one our children may not have yet discovered. To our children, all things are possible.

Many studies have been done on the benefits of positive thinking. "There are only two ways to live your life," Einstein said. "One is as though nothing is a miracle. The other is as though everything is a miracle." When people routinely gravitate toward possibility and hope, they often find it. In times of darkness, believing that the light is around the corner, they are resilient. I believe that this is not only a learned optimism, although optimism can and should be practiced; I believe that this is our natural state. What is more evidence of this than our children trying again and again when they are learning to walk? Trying again is, in itself, an act of faith.

When I teach, I often take my students through an exercise designed to uncover their own creative desires. "Blank piece of paper," I tell them. "Now list ten things you love to do but do not allow yourself to do." The lists are varied. "Lie out in the sun," one person ventures. "Go out and get an ice cream cone for no reason," another one chimes in. "Sing in public," says another. "Sing in the shower!" a fourth says with a laugh. When we do this exercise, we often discover that there are many small joys we are denying ourselves that we could, in fact, enjoy. In exploring our own desires, we become more free. In becoming more free ourselves, we grant more freedom to our children.

Watching our children play, creating castles from sand or stables from books, we must allow our children their spiritual, creative experience. Worrying obsessively about how they will perform at their interview for preschool or whether they are listening to enough classical music, we turn them away from their own inventiveness. That inventiveness, which is unique and innate in every person, is the very thing that will lead them to experience a certain magic and, very often, what also sets them apart and ultimately helps them to excel and achieve their goals.

SPONTANEOUS CREATION
An Exercise

Tell your child a story. It can be real or made up, something from your life or someone else's.

When you are done, ask your child to tell you a story. If necessary, give your child a simple prompt. "Tell me a story about a pony," you may say, or "Tell me a story about your doll." If your child has a favorite book, ask what happened before that story began, or after it ended. Listen attentively. Did your child's story surprise, inspire, please you? Be open to the magic of what children will create.

TRY EVERYTHING

Children explore all art forms. One day they may draw; the next day they may sculpt in clay; a day later and they're making music or playing dress-up. As parents, it falls to us to praise all of their efforts. We may have a favorite art form, but we serve our children best by displaying no favoritism.

As often as we can, and as openly as we can, we must expose our children to the art forms available to them and allow them to explore, uninhibited. If we despised learning the clarinet in school because of a passionless teacher, that is not a reason to avoid the clarinet with our own children. Giving gifts of toy instruments to children as young as toddlers is an inexpensive and fun way to determine where their inclinations may lie. Taking them to the local children's theater or art museum, we let them take in, without judgment, the many areas in which they, too, may wish to be creative. Handing them tools to draw, to sculpt, to make music, or to make up stories, we can observe the directions they gravitate toward and encourage their continued interest. Rarely does a child display a lifelong passion from the get-go, although it is not unheard of. More often, children dabble before committing. And even then, their interests will continue to change and morph. As we allow this natural progression of their interests, taking care not to insert our own buried dreams into their path, we clear a path for them to discover their own means of self-expression.

"My older daughter, Chloe, loves and excels in theater," said Peggy. "But my younger one, Brea, seems to be interested in everything. I'm not sure where to start, or how to focus with her. So I let her pick a couple of activities each season, and I guess we'll see what sticks." Peggy took Brea to soccer, to ballet, to painting classes and violin lessons. She took her to the symphony, to the circus, to plays and musicals. "I don't know," Peggy confessed to me. "I can't tell what she loves the way I could tell immediately with Chloe. Maybe it will expose itself later on."

Peggy continued Brea's general education, encouraging her in school and letting her know that any activity that her older sister participated in was also fair game for Brea. And then one day, at age eight, out of the blue, Brea began singing along with the radio. Loudly. "Her voice is huge," Peggy told me. "I had no idea!" Brea kept singing along with the pop songs she learned from the TV and radio, delighting her family with her raw talent and naturally strong voice. "I don't know where she learned this kind of breath control," Peggy said. "I didn't even know she could sing!" She enrolled Brea in voice lessons, and Brea is now excitedly learning more technique. She has already sung in front of her entire school. "I was so nervous in the audience," Peggy said. "But Brea was fine up there. She didn't seem nervous at all. I guess she's found what she likes."

Some children show us their interests more quickly than others. Some, like Brea, try many things before landing on something they truly desire to pursue. It is no surprise to me that Brea eventually found an artistic outlet, though. Peggy had set the stage for her to do so. With her gentle encouragement to "try anything," Peggy taught Brea not only that she didn't have to know what she loved immediately, but also that it was safe—and good—to experiment. No wonder that Brea is happy to stand up in front of her school and belt an Adele song into a microphone—a cappella, I might add. Her overall creativity was encouraged but not pressured. And when she did find her passion, it was allowed to come forth naturally. Finding her voice, Brea also found her own power and a piece of her identity.

As we seek to encourage our children in all directions, our telltale enthusiasms may creep through, despite our good intentions. I loved horses, and I was enthusiastic about Domenica's herd of toy horses. I taught her to hold the reins correctly on her stick horse. On the other hand, I had to work at my enthusiasm for her musical efforts. In my household, I was the "un-musical" member of my family. My brothers claimed the piano—quite virtuosically, I might add—and I was more often reading or typing away, writing short stories in my bedroom. I gravitated to other things, realizing only later that I, too, had a passion for musical composition. And so, aware that Domenica deserved to play with music, too, I helped her build a drum out of an oatmeal container. She patted out rhythms, and I praised her efforts. She sang, and I sang along with her. We listened to the Beatles and the Rolling Stones, danced and learned the lyrics. And when she was a teenager, I wrote the lead in my musical for her.

Showing our children that they have the ability—and the right—to experiment in all art forms, we teach them that they have choices. We teach them to try new things without over-thinking the consequences. Because there is no wrong way to experiment with a burgeoning creative endeavor, there is no judgment, no harsh consequence to follow. In the many people I have observed and the many interviews I have done with children who grew into creatively free adults, the most consistent story I hear is one of a parent who encourages early efforts. It is the attempt more than the product that we must champion. Artists are like athletes, returning again and again to practice. Teaching our children to practice experimenting, we teach them

to charge into the world with optimism and faith in their ability to begin anew.

EXPLORATION
An Exercise

Take pen in hand. List five creative endeavors you could encourage your child to try. Put no pressure on the result of these efforts—the idea is just to put a toe in the water and see how it feels.

1. _____

_____

2. _____

_____

3. _____

_____

4. _____

_____

5. _____

_____

Now list five creative endeavors you could try. These needn't be time-consuming or expensive. They should simply take you slightly out of your comfort zone. For example:

I could buy colored pencils and draw the flowers in my
neighbor's window box.
I could write a poem.

I could sing a song for my child, even though I don't
think I can sing.

1. _____

   _____

2. _____

   _____

3. _____

   _____

4. _____

   _____

5. _____

   _____

Choose one item from your child's list and one from
your own. Try them.

DOCUMENTATION

On my dining room table, I have a picture of my daughter, Domenica, and her husband, Tony. In the picture, they gleefully hold
aloft their marriage license. I treasure the picture and treasure the
moment it represents. Close at hand is another photo, this one of
Domenica and me, taken at a restaurant just before she announced
her engagement. This moment, too, is a treasure.

Documenting our memorable moments is a pastime that can
begin when your child is very young. I have two more photos of
Domenica that I cherish. In one, she is two years old and she is

seated atop a spotted pony while I lead her around the ring in Griffith Park, Los Angeles. In the second photo, Domenica is five. She is seated on her very first pony, Silver Lily, and her father stands just to one side, smiling proudly. Both of these photos belong in Domenica's scrapbook—or, if you will, her memory book. A photo says, "Yes, this memory really happened."

Now that we have digital cameras and the capacity to print photos at home, scrapbooks are easier to assemble. Not all of Domenica's snapshots involve horses, but a great many of them do. Here she is at age seven, riding my sister's mare Splash, bareback and no-handed. Horseback riding is a passion that we share and an art that she nurtures in her adult life. I suspect that it is a skill and enthusiasm that she will pass on to her own children as well.

As play becomes art becomes memories, we pay homage to our children's creative endeavors. Six-year-old Brynne paints daily, adding to her large collection of works of art. "Her favorite pastime is creating huge, colorful paintings," says her mother, Lidie. "I've taught her how to clean out the brushes when she's done. She feels like a professional, setting up her paints and her easel each day, and taking care of her supplies 'like a real painter,' she says." Brynne's collection grows weekly, and some of the pieces are especially beautiful. "She's very proud of them," Lidie tells me. "And so am I—they're amazing, some of them." Lidie decided that it was time to create a sort of "gallery" for the fruits of Brynne's labors. Lidie and Brynne took a trip to the craft store, choosing shimmering pink cardboard with which to cut out large letters. She hung the words "My Masterpieces" on Brynne's playroom wall, and now has a rotating gallery of Brynne's current favorites.

"We change the collection when we feel like it," Brynne tells me. "When I paint something really good, I put it up and choose which one will come down. Just like a real gallery." Brynne proudly leads me through her art museum, pointing out details of her paintings and explaining their origins and inspirations. As the curator of her playroom, Brynne is empowered and inspired. As Lidie continues to support her efforts by providing a beautifully designed display for Brynne's art, she encourages energetic continuation of Brynne's efforts. By documenting and acknowledging the art that our children create, we empower the precious fountain of creativity that exists within every child.

We live in a time when documentation is easier than ever before. Taking digital photos and uploading them to Facebook is an almost-instantaneous process that garners "likes" from our friends within moments. We can now share our children's development and interests with friends far and wide, and observe their lives as well. Keeping a camera or cell phone in our purse or pocket, we are able to seize the moment in a casual and everyday way that ultimately builds a cherished canon of memories.

Today, Domenica and I look back over the photo albums we built together when she was a child. In one photo, she stands atop my shoulders wearing a party hat and grinning wildly. That party is for my friend Marissa's daughter, Starlight. In the very next shot, Starlight is opening her presents. Domenica gave her a stick horse. The third photo shows Domenica guiding Starlight's hands as she learns to hold the reins correctly. And in photo number four, Starlight is riding the stick horse as Domenica cheers her on.

Taking the time and trouble to make a scrapbook or photo album tells our children that the events of their life do matter. Gluing or taping images, we create a storybook, and our children are the stars. Now that Domenica is grown, she cherishes the photos of her childhood adventures. They give her a sense of continuity. Here's a picture of Joanie, and one of Doris. She's still in touch with both women, thirty years later.

"Look at Calla Lily," Domenica will exclaim, singling out a photo of our snow-white standard poodle. "She was the best dog."

The time and attention that it takes to assemble a scrapbook or photo album pays off not only for our children but for ourselves as well. After all, memory can be fleeting. Freezing the moments in time guarantees that we will not forget.

CAPTURING MEMORIES

An Exercise

Today, choose a moment, activity, or work of art to document.

Then allow your child to take a photo of her own, allowing her, too, to choose the moments that will last forever. Digital cameras provide us endless possibilities for viewing. We can upload the pictures to our computer, using them as screen savers. We can buy an electronic photo frame that loops through our memories. As we add to our collection, we can add them to the rotation, wherever we display it. Seeing the collection grow, we—and our children—relive and recherish the memories, inspiring us all to create more.

Chapter Six

CULTIVATING INVENTIVENESS

~

The very act of creation might be defined as inventing something new, making something from nothing. Mining the daily realities of our lives for creative opportunities, we teach our children to do the same. We can find fun in unlikely places as we approach seemingly humdrum activities with joy and imagination. Dealing with boredom and menial tasks, we can actively choose to bring a sense of play. Exposing our children, in bite-sized increments, to the adult realities of running a household, we can pique their interest and help them to value—and enjoy—money earned and goals accomplished. Consciously digging deeper and setting an example of innovation, we learn—and teach—that within every activity, however simple, can lie inspiration.

THE BOREDOM MYTH

"I'm bored," our children complain, and the look in their eye completes the unspoken end of their sentence: "Fix it."

The idea that "boredom" is a stagnant state in and of itself is a myth. Boredom has nothing to do with stasis. It is, in fact, the opposite. Boredom is a call to action, a prompt to change direction. Boredom does not mean we are "out of ideas." It means we are ready to move on to the next one. Because creativity is an indwelling force infusing all of life, it is a constant supply that is available to us at every moment.

As a child, I lived in a home richly endowed with playthings and pastimes. In my after-school playtime, I had ample choices of things that would engage my attention. And yet I would sometimes announce to my mother, "I'm bored." My mother had a quick comeback: "If you're bored, it's because you lack inner resources." My mother was not about to be bullied. She knew she had placed multiple toys at my disposal. I remember being angry that I couldn't guilt-trip her into providing still more pastimes. After all, I could draw, build with blocks, play with clay, do dress-up, or herd my toy animals. Far from bored, my only real difficulty lay in choosing the day's delight. Multiple toys encourage multiple interests. There is no place for boredom in a well-stocked playroom.

Claire, a comedienne, tells me of her stepmother's quick comeback to her complaints of boredom. "Oh, good!" she would say. "Because I have a list of chores for you to do!"

"My brothers and I quickly learned to never say we were bored," Claire says, and chuckles. "Otherwise, we'd be stuck doing the most boring chores of all! My stepmother always had a list ready to go—polishing the silverware, raking the lawn, dusting the baseboards. By learning not to say 'I'm bored,' we learned to change focus."

Growing up in rural France, Claire found many of her pastimes were outdoors. Picking flowers or exploring the edges of her parents' property, she would make up stories of elves living in the trees and the journey a bird had taken before deciding where to settle and build her nest.

"There wasn't a lot of artificial stimulus in my childhood," Claire remembers. "TV was strictly limited, as was mindless computer time. So we used our imaginations a lot."

"Using" imagination is a more literal expression than we may realize at first glance. Imagination is a part of all of us, as available to us as thought itself. Using it, we exercise an important muscle. Strengthening that muscle, we develop the empowering habit of exercising the part of our brain that is the most original and most individual to us.

It is easy to fall into negative habits of complaining, of looking through a pessimistic lens at the world, of nitpicking, of seeing ourselves as victims. When we consciously push ourselves to look for imaginative solutions, we are granted optimism and inspiration. When we leave our children to their own devices, allowing them to rely "only" on their imaginations, we offer them the same reward. Engaging the world imaginatively, in large and small ways, we are at a distinct advantage. While boredom asks us to dally, we must instead stubbornly take this boredom as a cue to change direction. Imagination urges us on toward our own True North.

In a time of overabundant stimulation and distraction available to us and our children at every moment, we have to be even more vigilant. Giving our children the time and space to come to their own conclusions and new ideas, we help them. Hovering and directing their every move, we hinder them. How will they learn to pick up a pen or a set of paints or a musical instrument and be self-starting if we do it for them? We must be careful that we are not teaching them *not* to think—or, worse, to be afraid to be alone with their thoughts, that vast emptiness of "what's next," which, paradoxically, is the source of true inspiration. By handing them every idea, we are teaching them that by complaining of boredom, they are granted a new idea in return. And this will never work, because the idea they are looking for is their own, not ours.

Feeling bored is inconvenient. It says, "Move on now. Look deeper. Push harder." We would rather not feel bored. The same is true of our children. The good news about a call to action is that it initiates progress in us. The bad news is that it requires that we make a change. It requires getting up and searching for new ideas when we may not be in the mood to search. We may wish to be numbed by television, the Internet, a slice of cake. Our children are no different. But ignoring the promptings of boredom and indulging in a mind-numbing activity only puts off the inevitable. Once we have been called to action, that call will not go away until we indeed act on it. We may try to bury it, avoid it, douse it with cold water, but it will not go away. The embers will not go out, and the stirring of our soul will not stop. This is the calling of our own creative spirit, a spirit that exists in every person. When we feel that we are bored, it is because we have something to say.

The next time your child complains of boredom, try to resist the temptation to "solve" it by offering another activity. Try, instead, to hear what they are really saying. What exactly are they bored by? What exactly are they done with? What change of direction is required?

BLASTING THROUGH BOREDOM
An Exercise

As quickly as you can, fill in the following sentence five times. If your child is old enough to tell you that he is bored, he is old enough to do this exercise as well. It may be done verbally or on paper. We are going for speed and the free-form variety of ideas that comes to us when we work quickly enough to outsmart the part of us that might try to second-guess our first impulses.

I could _____.

I could _____.

I could _____.

I could _____.

I could _____.

DEALING WITH THE DREADED

"In every job that must be done, there is an element of fun," caroled Mary Poppins. In dealing with the dreaded, it is time to look to our own creativity to help our children participate in and accept some of the more humdrum daily routines and responsibilities of life. When we do, we show them that fun can be made anywhere and everywhere. Experiencing this will go a long way toward cultivating their enjoyment of small things, and as a result, their overall productivity and effectiveness. In learning to deal with the dreaded in a positive way, we eliminate roadblocks to success before they even exist.

Not every day can be a play day. Inevitably, there will arise those days when work demands our attention. Perhaps we have laundry left to fold or a trip to the grocery store. It falls to us to engage our children's imagination, to make a game out of the tasks at hand. For laundry, we can have our children identify the owner of each piece we fold. "That's mine!" "That's Daddy's!" "That's yours!" As stacks build up, so will the desire to sort even more. Grocery shopping also calls on your child's powers of concentration. Begin at the outer edge and work in concentric circles. Start off with fruits and vegetables; finish with baking supplies. Engage your child in choosing. "We love to play the alphabet game," Sara says, encouraging her son to look for the letters on the labels. Talking to your children about where different foods come from can be an educational and interesting way to pass the necessary time in the grocery store.

Everyday tasks such as picking up toys, taking a bath, and getting ready for bed can also be livened up. "Seventy-two Pickup" is a good way to turn cleanup time into a game. For the bath, try an extra squirt of bubbles, yielding festive froth. At bedtime, allow your child to choose the evening's reading. All of these playful stratagems work to transform drudgery to fun.

Larger endeavors arise as well, and, planning ahead, we can ensure that these yield pleasant memories, too.

Ginger tells the story of growing up in New Hampshire and visiting her grandmother and cousins every summer. She, her parents, and her brother would pack up the car and take the twenty-hour cross-country drive to Illinois to go to Granny's house.

"In hindsight, it was quite an undertaking," Ginger tells me now. "Twenty hours in the car with two little kids?" But the family had their rituals, and in the end, every element of the trip was anticipated with excitement.

On the day the trip began, they would leave at four a.m., "to get a good head start." It was an adventure to be awoken at three-thirty, when it was still dark and sleep hung in the cool outdoor air. "The car was packed the night before," Ginger explained, "so that we could get right in and start driving." The back of the car was set up with sleeping bags and pillows, and the kids looked forward to nestling deep into their cozy spots and watching out the window as the sun rose on the day.

"Going to Granny's house was a huge highlight," Ginger said. "She baked special cookies for her grandkids, which she stored high on a shelf in a white cookie jar. She lived on Lake Michigan, and we would swim in the lake and play in the sand. Her garden was filled with flowers, and we loved exploring our mom's old childhood toys in the house. There was a lot to look forward to, and we could hardly sleep as we imagined the visit to come."

Ginger's health-conscious parents made an exception on the way to Granny's house: the family would go to a fast-food restaurant for breakfast on the first day of driving, and all of them could order anything they wanted. "I always got pancakes," Ginger tells me. "It was a huge treat!" As the trip went on, stops along the way in foreign towns captured their imagination. They pulled into a campground and set up a tent at night, dragging sleeping bags from the car and reading with flashlights in the dark. In the morning, the shower in the main cabin was cool and exotic in the wooden-walled structure. "Everything about the trip was different from being at home," she remembers.

Although they drove two long days, the trip always seemed to pass quickly. With something new around every corner, and the promise of Granny in a matter of hours, they enjoyed their journey. To break up the monotony, their mother would have "present time" along the way, pulling a new game or a book from her bag and delivering it to the backseat, where Ginger and her brother would excitedly explore the new gift.

After their week with Granny, when the time came to begin the long drive back home, Granny would present "Granny Bags" to each grandchild. Gift bags adorned with Miss Piggy and Kermit signaled the girls' and boys' stashes. For each hour that each child would be in the car, there was a small gift. "One an hour," Granny would say, handing them the bag.

"It was like magic," Ginger says. "Once every hour in the car, we got to pull an item from the Granny Bag. There might be a small jar of M&M's, or a toy or a game. There might be a special pen or a set of stickers. It made the hours fly by. The mystery of what we would pull out next consumed us, and the magic of Granny was with us there in the car."

As much as we can, we must teach our children that even the most mundane jobs can be turned to fun. Children love to turn everyday events into games. Setting a timer for cleanup, sorting laundry into "whose's whose" piles, being in charge of drying dishes or putting away silverware—if we can make the job fun, our children will willingly join in.

AN ELEMENT OF FUN
An Exercise

List your five most dreaded activities.

1. _____
   _____

2. _____
   _____

3. _____
   _____

4. _____
   _____

5. _____
   _____

Now, next to each one, see if you can think of a way to insert a little fun. For example, if one of your dreaded activities is "grocery shopping, because my son begs for candy," perhaps you can agree to choose a small treat together, such as a new magnet or other small non-food item available in the grocery store, so long as your child holds up his end of the behavioral deal (no begging for candy). Succeeding, you will both be rewarded with a sense of pride, a successful trip to the store to build on for next time, and an anticipated treat.

THE VALUE OF MONEY

Few tasks are more satisfying—or essential—than teaching our children the value of money. When you take a creative approach, it can also be great fun. A weekly allowance and a piggy bank are the places to start. A quarter, a dime, a nickel, a penny. Each coin has its value. Assigning tasks that allow your children to earn money helps them to understand the idea that money is an exchange of energy. Not all tasks should involve a monetary payoff; children need to learn to pitch in as working members of the household. But cash can be a valuable incentive when the tasks at hand are above and beyond the call of duty. Cleaning their bedrooms and helping with groceries may be expected responsibilities, but other tasks, such as weeding the garden, might pay a small fee. Monies earned can be monies saved as the piggy bank begins to have some heft. Once a month, the piggy bank can be emptied and coins counted. "You see? You have enough money to buy yourself a treat." Saving for two months might yield enough cash to buy a coveted toy, or your child can choose to save it instead.

When she wasn't buying us flowers, Domenica's money went toward toy horses. Her friend Simone bought doll clothes. Learning to pay cash on the barrelhead, children learn to value every cent. Having their own money gives them a sense of power and helps them to appreciate when parental money is spent on their behalf. Money in, money out, children learn to appreciate a bargain. They learn, too, when something is overpriced and they cannot afford it. It is important that parents set the allowance or the job fee at the right amount. Too much money for too little work is as damaging as too little money for too much work. It is important to find stores where your child's allowance has real buying power. A grocery store or a five-and-dime do nicely. "What do you want to buy today?" you may ask your children. Don't be too discouraged if the answer is "M&M's."

Many children who were raised to be creative speak of growing up with very little money. A composer friend of mine practiced piano on a toy keyboard until his parents could afford to buy a used piano for him to play on. "It's an old piano, but it works," he says of the instrument, which is still in his parents' living room. "It's usually out of tune, and there's plenty wrong with it. But I cherished it when they got it, and I cherish it today. I wrote my first fifty songs on that piano. I practiced for hours, determined to learn every chord in the jazz vocabulary, to be able to play them in every key and identify them by ear, on cue. I reached these goals." My friend grew up in a small town, studying piano with "a crazy old guy who taught lessons at the piano store for seven dollars an hour." But my friend was passionate, and so was his teacher. He didn't need a pristine ballroom with a Steinway piano to learn chords and write songs. He didn't need to go to a conservatory to gain knowledge of music during high school. He simply needed to chase his passions. Today, my friend has written several hit pop songs. And now, he does indeed own a beautiful piano.

"Once I started making money, I bought myself a grand piano," he tells me. For him, money is no longer an issue. "It feels like a huge splurge, and I do love it. What a luxury to walk into my Manhattan apartment and see this dramatic instrument that is my very own. But that's really what it is—a luxury. It's not a necessity for me. Songs can be written in the back of a cab or on the subway. I sing them into my phone and go home and write them down. It often seems that my best ideas come to me when I'm in the most mundane places."

My composer friend tells me that he later met colleagues who grew up in more privileged circumstances than he. To his eye, he is the one with the advantage. "I learned from my parents that if you worked hard, you could achieve your dream. I also learned that I could write songs on a keyboard as well as writing on a piano. I even learned to write in my head. It's more about wanting to write a song than the beauty of the room in which you do it. As I met friends in college who came from wealthy backgrounds, I noticed that they seemed less joyful about their activities, and less childlike overall. It's like they had seen it all already, and there wasn't a lot of magic left for them."

Regardless of a parent's level of financial resources, they can encourage artistry in their children. Making art rarely costs us much, if anything. There are expensive and inexpensive ways to pursue artistic education, and if a parent is willing to research and budget their options for supporting the true interests of their child, they are bound to succeed, whether they are in a world-class urban training environment or choosing the right piano teacher for their particular child at the local piano shop. As parents spend money wisely, encouraging clear artistic values rather than the accoutrements of an artistic lifestyle, children learn to do the same.

Giving our children the example of how to spend money consciously, and giving them the opportunity to earn money—be it pocket change through chores or larger rewards for larger jobs—we empower our children to understand that they have earning power and choice. Learning to save money and to spend it, they are learning to assign value to items they desire. "Is this one worth the money?" they must ask themselves when they have only enough cash to choose one item. Making the wrong choice is good for them, too. Coming home only to wish they had bought the toy their brother bought, or chosen the doll that they had left behind, they can decide to do things differently next time. Learning to spend along our true values, be it spending hard-earned allowance money or spending money toward our children's education, is a skill we must all hone by trial and error. It is good to begin young; beginning young, we ingrain a prosperity consciousness—the art of right spending—that will carry our children far and help protect their finances in the future.

EARNING MONEY
An Exercise

To experience the joys of long-term planning, see if you can create a large creative goal for your child. As the child accomplishes a baby step (for example, practicing the violin for one hour), allow him to "earn" a quarter, a dollar, or whatever you determine to be fair. Let him know he can "cash in" only at certain landmarks (fifty hours practiced, for instance). This playful motivator has worked wonders for many a project. Allow your child to decorate the chart, and proudly display it with the goal and his progress clearly marked.

THE CULINARY KINGDOM

Food is a major part of family time and larger family gatherings, and allowing your children to participate in the "family-style" activity of meal preparation is a gesture of trust, confidence, and interest that is likely to be not only appreciated but also enjoyed by your children. Being a part of the process, children see where the meal came from on its way to their plate. They may recognize ingredients they helped you shop for or choose vegetables from the garden that perhaps they themselves have planted. Children become empowered as they learn to cook for themselves and others.

When they are as young as age two, we can allow our toddlers to tear up lettuce for salad. We can invite our young children to set the table, allowing them to labor over one utensil at a time as they carefully prepare each place. We can encourage their efforts, and let them become invested in the meal that is to come. "I made that," they proudly announce as the salad is passed. "I folded those napkins." As they feel a sense of ownership over what is being served and how, they learn to care about food and what goes into creating it.

Katherine is an inspiring aunt to more than a dozen nieces and nephews. Her home, with its sprawling kitchen, is a natural gathering place. Her relatives are as drawn to her loving, open-door attitude as they are to her spectacular cooking. Harvesting a large garden, she often grows the foods that wind up on her dinner table.

"I let the kids help me as young as age three," she says. "They can help as a salad chef, a sous-chef, or a dessert chef. I let them choose how they are going to participate and then show them the ropes within the area they've picked." I watch Katherine coach the youngest, a delicate, brown-eyed beauty, as she places blueberries, strawberries, and raspberries into bowls filled with fluffy slices of angel food cake.

"I'm a dessert chef," her niece announces to me.

"I see," I agree.

Katherine guides her niece's small hand as she ladles raspberry compote into each dish.

"Looks delicious," I observe.

Katherine has several of the older children chopping vegetables. I'm impressed with their technique, and I tell her as much.

"Practice." Katherine grins at me.

Before my eyes, her small army produces a large and festive meal. The table is set, salad and crudités are prepared, bread is sliced, olive oil is drizzled. Fresh herbs from Katherine's garden garnish the salad and chicken that her husband carries in from the outdoor grill. I can see why Katherine's house is a destination. There is a freedom in her kitchen. Spills are matter-of-factly cleaned up. Collisions among sous chefs are laughed off. And in the end, the pride in the group effort fills the air as much as the aromatic dishes.

Over dinner, her oldest nephew talks about the Italian olive oil on Katherine's table with such passion that I ask him if he might want to go to culinary school or study cooking in some way. "I would," he confirms. "And I have to go to Italy. That's my first goal. I want to know where the best olive oil in the world comes from, and I need to go and test them all to find out. I'd like to find the olive oil that I consider perfect, and bring it to the

U.S. Maybe I can even start some kind of business when I get out of school." I study him as he speaks, believing he may well do just that.

Katherine is a truly gifted chef, but her gift of generosity is perhaps even more impressive. There is a sense of safety and experimentation in her kitchen. "I want them to be invested in the meal," she says. "It encourages creativity and good table manners to have them participate." She glances around her countertops at the open containers and remnants of the cooking endeavor. "However, this process can cause extreme messiness," she says, smiling, "so adults have to know going in that they'll need to leave the critical parent in them behind."

I agree with her, thinking that she has just summed up, in one sentence, the reason I wanted to write this book.

Inviting your child to cook with you as part of his afterschool playtime expands his creativity. Simple recipes are best. My mother taught each of her seven children the rudiments of cooking. She explained as she went. "Tonight we're going to make a tuna casserole. The ingredients are tuna fish, potato chips, mushroom soup, and peas." She showed us how to crush the potato chips, lay down a layer, spread the tuna fish, spread the mushroom soup, and add canned baby peas. Next, another layer, and she repeated the ingredients. Finally, she added a last layer of chips and drizzled the casserole with milk. While the casserole was baking at 350 degrees, it would be time to set the table. This, too, could be fun. Placing the silverware on the correct side of the plate, getting the glassware and setting it to the right, putting out the salt and pepper, the bread and butter, the jam. These were all simple tasks that would be rewarded with the exclamation "Good job!"

When the dinner was served, my mother always made a point of complimenting her co-chefs.

Dorothy taught her children to make comfort food. I, in turn, taught Domenica. It was with great pride that she prepared a large pot of chili to feed her film crew. "They loved it, Mommy!" she reported gleefully. Tuna casserole was next up, with homemade cherry pie for dessert. The pie featured a crisscross lattice top that made it look fancy. Domenica learned the intricacies of pie making at my elbow. Including your child in your cooking accomplishes two valuable things: it provides a sense of pride in the present, and it promises autonomy in the future.

COOK SOMETHING
An Exercise

Whether you consider yourself a gourmet chef or a total beginner in the kitchen, there is a recipe that you can make with your child. Choose something appropriate for both of you, then create your dish together, from shopping to cleanup. Allow your child to participate and be "in charge" of appropriate steps. Notice the ownership you both feel when you are enjoying the meal or snack together, and congratulate yourselves on a job well done.

Chapter Seven

CULTIVATING CONSCIOUS INFLOW

~

Our children's creativity has two pulses: outflow and inflow. Our children are enriched by the world around them, and we can—and must—take care to choose positive stimulation for our children. Exposing them to many art forms, from woodworking to drawing to playing music to writing, they find rich avenues for self-expression. As we encourage positive imagery about artists, we must be consciously aware of our own assumptions about creativity and take care to pass on open and accepting values. Exposing our children to art forms of all stripes, we help them form passions and opinions as they form themselves.

ARTISTS ARE . . .

When it comes to our children's creativity, many of us fall into unconscious beliefs that we may have about artists. We must be willing to examine these negative beliefs so as not to unwittingly pass them on to our developing children.

When I teach creative unblocking, one of the first exercises we do is called "Archaeology." This examines the beliefs we were taught as children related to creativity. "Fill in the blank," I prompt my class. "My mother thought artists were . . ."

The room erupts with answers, and those answers seem to be the same, regardless of what country or demographic I am teaching in.

"My mother thought artists were weird!" someone will call out.

"Mine thought artists didn't have real jobs!"

"My mother thought artists were geniuses!"

I will urge them to fill in the blank again. "My father thought artists were . . ."

"My father thought artists were all broke."

"My father thought artists would never have families."

"My father thought artists were the most important people in the world."

Examining the beliefs passed on to us from our parents, we gain insight into our own beliefs about artists. There are also the more general societal misconceptions and assumptions about artists.

I now guide my class in another exercise: "Fill in the blank. Artists are . . ."

Lonely, broke, crazy, selfish, brilliant, famous, generous . . .

the list goes on and on. Neither the negative nor the positive assumptions are necessarily true, and both can be damaging. If artists are indeed lonely, crazy, drug-addicted, and unstable, we certainly don't want to rush right out and become artists—or encourage our children to. If artists, on the other hand, are famous, brilliant, generous, rich . . . well, on the mornings when we wake up feeling famous, brilliant, generous, and rich, we qualify—by our own definition—to be artists.

The truth is much less dramatic. Artists are people who make art. Some do it professionally. Some do it for fun. Some are famous, some are lonely; some are happily married, some are single. As in any other profession, artists are human, with a range of human experiences.

We must be conscious of our own default beliefs when speaking to our children about creativity. Every person is creative. Every child is in touch with that creativity. Every child deserves to be encouraged in the direction of their creative interests. We must respect the creativity in ourselves and others, and respect creativity itself.

Another trap that parents can fall into is making—and voicing—assumptions about their own creativity.

"I'm not very creative," we may hear ourselves saying when our children ask us to make up a story or show them how to draw a dog. "I'm not really artistic," we say casually when our children beg us to go to the art supply store and ask for guidance in choosing the type of paints to buy.

Every person is creative. Creativity is the natural order of life. When we tell our children that we are not creative, our children learn that there is such a thing as "not being creative," which is deeply untrue. Once they have this (mis)information, it is a short walk to their repeating it about themselves. You are creative. Your child is creative. Encouraging that in both of you opens doors to happiness, connection, and, yes, increased performance and ability in other areas.

Be thoughtful when you speak of artists to your children. Be thoughtful when you respond to their art, and be thoughtful when you discuss your own. You do not have to be a professional oil painter to help your child enjoy painting. Allowing them to experiment with a set of watercolors is a gesture of faith and encouragement. Allowing yourself to join in is an even greater one. You do not have to paint a perfect dog. You can paint a messy dog in neon pink because you secretly love neon pink, and your child will be better for it. And so, I predict, will you. As long as you are willing to say, "This looks fun. I'd like to try this, too," your child will mimic your example of openness, playfulness, and optimism.

DEBUNKING MYTHOLOGY
An Exercise

Fill in the following sentence ten times:

Artists are _____.

Look at your answers. Do you believe that artists are crazy, broke, negative? Do you believe that they are powerful, brilliant, and kind? Don't judge your answers. This is simply a sleuthing exercise. Being aware of the mythology you personally carry in relation to assumptions about artists, you are more able to communicate positively with your child about the value of creativity.

READING

Reading to—and with—our children is one of the most time-honored traditions of parenting. Looking back to our own childhoods, many of us remember a favorite book and a time when it was read to us. Following along, we came to see that the letters created words and that—voilà!—reading was something we, too, could learn to do. Our favorite childhood stories stay with us, often foreshadowing interests to come and influencing us in larger ways than we might realize. Becoming a part of our subconscious, the messages in these books nestle deeply in our psyche, shaping our values and clarifying our interests.

The age-old ritual of nightly reading helps to establish the bedroom as a special place. Your child's imagination takes wing when you read them a nightly story.

"It's story time," my mother would exclaim, leading the way to the bedroom. "Let's get our jammies on first." And then it would be time to launch into a beloved story—*Little Toot* or *Green Eggs and Ham*. "Hop in bed now," she would instruct before taking up her position alongside. Reading needn't last a long time. What is important is the consistency of the nightly ritual.

In the Cameron house, there was a complete set of the My Book House books, a twelve-volume anthology of children's literature featuring poems, mythology, fairy tales, and folk tales, and wonderful illustrations. "It's always a pleasure to get a Cameron child," remarked Sister Carl, our favorite teacher. "Your mother does such a good job with you. You're already educated." Our mother would read from a volume nightly, beginning with *Mother Goose*, working up to *Beowulf*. In addition to the Book House books, she read to us from Marguerite Henry: *Misty of Chincoteague, Sea Star, Brighty of the Grand Canyon*, and more. In time, we learned that the words stood for ideas. P-O-N-Y equaled "pony"; B-A-L-L equaled "ball." The evening's reading was enticing. We always wanted more. But our mother kept the reading ritual to fifteen minutes—a perfect amount of time for both parent and child. Although we did not actually learn to read until we went to school, we learned the idea of reading, that words on the page added up to whole stories, from our nightly bedtime routine.

In time, all of us became voracious readers. In our hall by the front coat closet, there were two heating grates. We would take a book and lie, tummy down, on the heaters, with the book propped just ahead of us on the rug. With bookshelves brimming with yet unread stories and a library down the street, there was a wide world awaiting our curious minds. To this day, my six siblings and I still count reading among our great pleasures. All of us have a book or two that we are reading at any given time. Several of us are now writers ourselves, and all of us would include literature high on our list of inspiring interests.

"It amazes me how many times my three-year-old daughter wants to read the same books," says Hank. "We'll get to the end of a book we've read hundreds of times, and she'll immediately say 'Again!'" Like revisiting an old friend, our children love to hear favorite stories over and over. It is thrilling for them to know what is coming. They are getting to know a work of art, mastering its intricacies. They are experiencing the excitement of knowledge.

"Reading was the activity that connected me to my best friend," says Sissy, now a highly trained governmental adviser. "I came from a big family, and so did my friend Sarah. Both of us were more serious than the others, and while our brothers were tearing the town apart on their bikes, climbing trees, and playing pranks on each other, Sarah and I would take our books to the roof of the barn and read where no one could bother us. We spent entire summers up there, and although there would be long stretches where we read, side by side, speaking very little, the experience bonded us for life. We are still there for each other to this day. Those summers made me know that it was okay to be bookish and that I wasn't alone. Somehow, Sarah is always sitting next to me when I read." Now living with several states between them, Sissy and Sarah are regularly in touch, and their friendship is as loyal as it was when they climbed onto the roof of the barn at age ten, backpacks filled with library books. "I don't know how many people can say that they are still close to their childhood best friend," Sissy remarks, "but I think reading side by side is a big part of how Sarah and I created a truly unbreakable bond."

Reading connects us to other people virtually, as well. We break our isolation when we read, as we connect with stories and ideas that we have not yet encountered. There is camaraderie in reading, and a sense of expansion of our own experience. Even when we are reading on our own, we are kept company by the characters in the story or the author's narrative voice. Reading, we are never alone. Sharing experiences through reading, we connect ourselves to something larger. Connecting to something larger, we become larger ourselves.

CHERISHED BOOKS

An Exercise

What was your favorite childhood book? Do you see the themes of this book in your life and values today? Can you give that book to your child?

Next choose a book that you would like to read now but that you feel you do not have time to read. When your child reads on his own, whether he is merely old enough to turn pages in a picture book or advanced enough to read silently by himself, allow yourself a few minutes to indulge in your own book. You will connect to each other in your common activity, and in the company of sharing that quiet time "together but separate."

MUSIC

Whether our children show a passion for creating music or if they just enjoy listening to it, we can encourage our children to be open musicians by playing all kinds of music in the house and encouraging every member of the family to be drawn to what they naturally enjoy. Brothers John and Matthew grew up in a home full of music. Their mother taught piano, and their father was an amateur trumpet player who often awakened the house with "revelry" at five o'clock in the morning. They regularly attended classical concerts by the local orchestra in their small town, and the house was often filled with the sounds of folk records by Judy Collins and Peter, Paul, and Mary. On Saturday mornings, their father would pull out his favorite album, *A Night at the Opera* by Queen, and blast it through the house as he did the weekly Saturday household chores. Their mother would roll her eyes at the volume of the record, but the boys enjoyed their father's passion for rock music and came to form a deep appreciation of Queen themselves.

Early on, both brothers started studying Suzuki violin. The basics of music were taught, and both excelled. While Matthew continued in a serious classical direction all the way through graduate school, John became interested in other genres while he was still in elementary school. Studying classical violin, he would spend hours in his room listening to jazz, rock, and funk. He began to decipher the different chord progressions and soon joined a band. Their parents were clear that practicing was nonnegotiable, but beyond that, they allowed their sons to pursue the musical routes that appealed to them.

"Both of my sons were very talented in music, and that was clear from a young age," says their mother. "I wanted to support their interest and develop their talents. And although I was excited that they seemed to have both passion and natural gifts, it was more important that they learn the value of hard work than anything else. Discipline is necessary in mastering any instrument. And because music came easily for both of them, that really carried with it a responsibility to work even harder. I don't think that the gift of talent means you get to do less. I think it actually requires that you do more. The bigger the potential, the harder you must work to try to reach it."

As both sons grew up, they entered lives as professional musicians. Matthew, who completed graduate work in classical cello performance, decided that pop music spoke to him more, and in his twenties, he began writing. Today, his songs are heard on the radio. John went more in the direction of performance, and has toured with many bands. Recently, John started a recording studio. "He's great at it," Matthew says of his brother's recording expertise. "He really has a sound. And I'm pretty sure that he was developing it in his room at age ten, playing those jazz records obsessively. He was learning how to listen."

Learning how to listen is the most important part of studying music and encouraging its place in our children's lives. Listening appreciatively to a new chord mastered on the guitar, we empower them to learn another. Praising their hard work, we encourage them to work hard anew. In music, as in any art form, it takes practice to move ahead. Encouraging their practice and participation motivates them to explore the many musical paths available to them.

Heather, a Broadway actress and singer, tells the story of her own music-friendly household. "From a very early age, it was clear that I had musical tendencies. At my second birthday party they had to drag me off the 'stage' of my living room when I wouldn't stop singing the ABCs into my plastic traffic-light microphone. When I was five, my mom started me on piano lessons, and even though all I wanted to do was play music from *The Little Mermaid* and *Beauty and the Beast*, I took to the piano and began to build a foundation of musicianship and theory. When fourth grade rolled around and we could choose any instrument to play in either the band or the orchestra, I picked the flute. I stuck with the flute and piano all the way through high school, giving me a leg up on other vocalists once I started my music degree in college. My mom also put me into a musical theater class when I was eight, beginning that whole spiral into the theater world. In a nutshell, my parents recognized my interest at an early age and made the right things happen to help develop my passions into talents. They have never made me feel like I need a 'backup plan,' instilling in me a confidence in my skills that has served me very well in this career of rejection. My parents have always believed in me, which has allowed me to believe in myself."

Looking at Heather's story, we can see that her inclinations to perform clearly foreshadowed her Broadway career. A stunningly talented actress and vocalist, it's difficult to imagine her taking any other path. But looking at her history, it was the encouragement of her parents that allowed her gifts to develop. All too often, children are shamed for singing too loud, for having a personality that is "too large," for "making noise on the piano" when a parent is trying to read the newspaper or watch TV. Letting our children's gifts and interests develop wherever they may lie, whether they are the same as ours or not, we give our children the chance to become themselves. For some of us, music is a passion to be pursued. For others of us, music is an integral part of life, and the latter is fine as well. Incorporating music into any life—whether by listening on the radio in the car or singing at church—is valuable. There is no right or wrong answer to the question "What is your favorite kind of music?" The right question—"What music do you enjoy?"—will lead to an answer that is always relevant and always changing.

LISTENING

An Exercise

Using CDs, iTunes, the radio, or whatever other music-listening device of your choice, listen to several contrasting types of music with your child. With each one, ask what your child thinks and feels about the style. Offer any knowledge you have—and it does not have to be much. A quick Google search can tell you that Beethoven wrote his Ninth Symphony a very long time ago, when he was completely deaf. It can tell you that Alicia Keys studied classical piano before releasing her first R&B album, *Songs in A Minor.* Your lesson can be minimal. The idea here is to offer, without judgment, exposure to several styles and eras of music. Allow your child to enjoy whatever he or she enjoys. There is no "wrong" kind of music to like.

BEING AN AUDIENCE

We teach our children to cherish creativity by cherishing it ourselves. We teach our children to respect the creative act by respecting it ourselves. This means we model not only making art ourselves but also appreciating the art made by others. We can start with the movies. There are many made for children's entertainment. We can attend, with child in tow, a big bag of popcorn to be shared, and an anticipation of quiet as we watch together. It won't be long before children learn that movies are quiet time, eyes focused on the screen. As we choose the movies with care, we get to know what interests our children and holds their attention. All children are different, and their actual proclivities may surprise us. If a film is "too adult," children will grow restless or become scared. "Too kiddy" and children become annoyed by being talked down to. If we miss and must abort the mission and leave halfway through, it is not the end of the world. Our children are learning the art of discernment.

I often tell the story of Domenica as a young child. I brought her to a movie that I thought might be a bit mature. She had seemed bored by more age-appropriate titles, so I decided to give this one a try. She sat silently beside me, not uttering a word through the entire movie. In her hand, her bag of M&M's lay untouched. She was focused completely on the screen.

As we left, I turned to her, seeking her thoughts on what we had seen. Had I taken her to something that might upset her? Was she a little too young for the story we had witnessed? When I asked for her opinion, she looked at me thoughtfully.

"It was only okay," she said. "I really don't think they should have killed the husband off-screen."

I laughed and told her I agreed. I didn't tell her that most seven-year-olds might not have quite that type of observation. Perhaps it is the moviemaker blood in her, the passion that she was born with, but whatever it was, I allowed it to be. We have gone to many more movies together over the years, and I continually find her insights enlightening.

Once our children have mastered the art of quiet moviegoing, with silent observation and questions postponed until later, it can be thrilling to graduate to viewing live performance. Theater is expensive and expansive, but carefully chosen, the expenditure is more than repaid. The colorful spectacle and catchy songs of *The Lion King* make it a favorite choice of mine. The story is simple enough to follow, and the villain easy enough to hate. If Broadway is out of reach, and it is for many of us, the local papers feature suggestions for child-friendly shows. An expedition to see *The Nutcracker* or a visit to view *Mary Poppins* in a nearby city can be enhanced by careful preparation. Introducing the children at home to the characters they'll be meeting in the theater helps to guarantee their respectful interest. Likewise, it's a good idea to familiarize them with the music they'll be hearing. You can download the Broadway cast album from iTunes before seeing the live show, whether it is a performance by a Broadway national tour or a local community theater.

I grew up on the tunes of Rodgers and Hammerstein, although I didn't see their shows until I was older. My mother was good at generating excitement. When Rodgers and Hammerstein crafted a television special of *Cinderella*, our mother made certain we were all glued to the set.

My best friend, Lynnie Lane, was a glorious singer. Her mother provided her with the cast albums of all the Rodgers and Hammerstein shows. She, in turn, spread the word by singing them to me. I still remember the thrill of hearing her carol "Climb Every Mountain." Listening to Lynnie, I learned to practice silence as golden. She trained me to be a good audience, a lesson I in turn would teach my daughter, Domenica.

We teach our children to be good audience members also by being an audience to them. When they present a story or work of art to us, our warm reception encourages them to continue to indulge their impulse to share. As we appreciate their efforts, they grow. As we sit back and enjoy the show without judgment or "correction," with no threat of trying to "improve on" their natural impulses, they grow more.

My performer friend Heather tells me the story of her early performances in her home: "When I was ten, we had an addition put on the back of our house, which meant that there were construction men all over our home every day. Without fail, and with no inhibitions, I would come home from school every single day, eat a snack, sit at the piano, and play and sing at the top of my lungs. I can only imagine what the construction workers thought. Probably that it was cute, hilarious, and *annoying* as hell. My mom, who was a stay-at-home mom, never once told me to stop or made me feel embarrassed. I had no knowledge that this didn't happen in every single house in our town."

Being an audience, we receive what is given to us. As we receive graciously, our children follow suit, learning to receive graciously themselves and to give generously as well.

IN THE AUDIENCE
An Exercise

Allow your child to perform for you or gift you with an artistic pursuit. See if you can name a specific quality that you appreciated in what he or she did. The more specific you can be, the better.

Now plan to take your child to be an audience member at a local event. It may be a high school or middle school

(continued)

concert, a gallery, a movie, a play. It doesn't matter what you choose. When you are done, ask your child to name something specific that they enjoyed or appreciated, and allow yourself to be surprised and fascinated by your child's answer.

STORYTELLING

We revisit our own stories as our children's stories are written. Sharing our favorite books and memories with them connects us to our past, present, and future. Our shared family history and culture are valuable pieces of identity for our children, and as we expose them to our backgrounds—and their own—we give them a context and structure in which to expand their own identity.

Our children are likely to make up "make-believe" stories, and we can also encourage them to tell autobiographical stories, even if it's just relating a funny incident from their school day. The point is to encourage their storytelling, and we do this first by prompting them, and then by listening.

We, too, can tell stories to our children, and the made-up kind may be intimidating for some of us. The most important thing to remember when our children ask us to "tell a story" is that this story does not have to be "good." We have to jump in anyway and try. Our children can help—we can ask what they think might happen next. We can use props, telling a story about their stuffed animals or toys. The point is that we set our own ego aside and be willing to begin.

My friend and colleague Tyler has taught storytelling for many years. "I think something becomes storytelling when there isn't a script," he tells me. "There's something special about that in a time where text is everywhere—books, movies, YouTube. We have an obsession with making a permanent record of everything, and the magic of storytelling is that it isn't like that. It only exists for a moment, between the teller and their audience." Much like live theater versus a movie, a story will be a little bit different every time, and there's always the possibility of the unexpected. With a live audience, whether the story is spontaneous or a retelling of a classic, the experience for the audience and the teller is new each time the story is told.

Storytelling is like a trip backward in time. Since the first humans sat around the fire, stories have been shared among people. Stories are passed on from one generation to the next, the thread of ancestry that connects us to our past and our future. Children love to hear stories from their parents' childhood, or stories of their grandparents' or great-grandparents' adventures.

"It's a primal urge," Tyler continues. "Because it's ultimately about safety. Every time. Even if we went back to the days of cavemen—let's say you are a caveman and another caveman told you a story about berries he ate that made him feel sick. You probably wouldn't eat them. Telling stories creates safety in your tribe."

In the tribe of our own family, storytelling works this same magic. Taking the time to talk—and to listen—binds us to each other. We may sit in the same room as someone else, both on laptops for hours. There is a certain company in that, but for the most part, our relationships are with our screens and not with one another. Storytelling is the opposite. It connects us as humans in a most ancient and basic way. Some of the best stories are just conversations. With one half telling and one half listening, both partners are active.

By sharing, we connect. By sharing, we define ourselves. Telling a story, we claim ownership over it. Encouraging others to do the same, we encourage their growth and independence as they name themselves and their experience.

Kiera, an actress, loves to tell stories to her three-year-old niece, Sondra, who absorbs the narratives with wonder. Kiera has spent many years performing in children's theater and as an improv comic, and her storytelling is something Sondra looks forward to on Kiera's frequent visits.

"I'm educating her in classic stories now," Kiera muses. "That's my current project. She needs to know all of them." Telling the story of Peter Pan to Sondra one day, Kiera acted out the different roles, and Sondra laughed hysterically at Kiera's many voices and accents. Explaining that "fairy dust" promises that Tinker Bell is nearby, Kiera told Sondra to keep an eye out for Tinker Bell after she'd left.

The next day, Kiera got a call from Sondra's mother.

"I was serving breakfast to her this morning, and she kept pointing to a spot in the corner of the ceiling. I finally realized she was saying that Tinker Bell was nearby. When I looked at what she was pointing at, it was a little spot of light reaching through the blinds. I thought you should know."

"Tell her that was absolutely Tinker Bell," Kiera said, laughing.

Her stories have sparked Sondra's imagination. Inspired to look for it, Sondra will continue to find magic throughout her world.

We certainly don't have to be professional actors or improv comics to tell our children stories. Simply giving them the raw material—the idea—is enough of a jumping-off point to trigger their vast imaginations.

"I love fairy tales," says Lillian. "I was obsessed with the Brothers Grimm and the old Disney movies as a child. And guess what? My daughter is going to be exposed to those things, too. We'll see if she loves them as much as I do, but not knowing about them isn't an option."

Lillian tells a story to her daughter every night before bed. Sometimes it is a known story; sometimes it is made up. "Inventing characters that my child might enjoy is fun for me, too," she says. "And the more I tell stories, the more comfortable I get with telling stories. It gets easier, whether I'm inventing a fairy tale or sharing an adventure of my own from when I was my daughter's age. The stories don't have to be perfect."

Story time can double as lesson time. Your characters can live and learn, just as your listening children can also learn. Often, our children have stories to tell, as well. Our job is simply to listen as our children continue the story that began long before us.

LISTENING

An Exercise

Experiment with telling a story to your child. It can be about anything, long or short. If you can't think of a topic, ask your child for a prompt. Perhaps it is about the flower on the windowsill or the dog at your feet. Perhaps it is about the invented life of the neighbor across the street or the passerby in the grocery store. There is no wrong topic.

When you are done, ask your child to tell you a story. Really listen to her. Did she have more to say than you might have guessed? Did you?

Chapter Eight

CULTIVATING FOCUS

~

When we are creatively active, we are in the moment. When we are in the moment, we are open and we are focused. There are many concrete steps we can take to improve our focus as well as our children's. With technology as a near-constant distraction, we must take even more care to nurture the important nutrients of our lives as well as our children's: good nutrition, physical activity, restful sleep, and spiritual health. A sound body and sound mind lead to a sound focus, and, learning this focus, our children are able—even likely—to create a sound body of creative work, play, and joy.

THE TECHNOLOGY EPIDEMIC

There is no substitute for the human imagination. We can invent stories and playful plots—that is, we can if we are given the time and mental space to do so. Far too many households, however, are overcrowded with technological paraphernalia. From the radio to the TV to the iPhone and iPad, the computer, and every new incarnation of video game, our children are swamped with high-tech distractions.

Timothy is addicted to video games. Their sound track is noisy and their plots violent. He kills off his enemies with mind-numbing explosions. His sole goal is to win, losing himself in mortar and mayhem. Connie has a favorite DVD. She begs her mother to play it "just one more time." It's not too severe to say that she's addicted. Her mother has misgivings, but she keeps them to herself. After all, she tells herself, the DVD is educational. For many parents, the proliferation of "gizmos" means less time for meaningful interaction with their children. Glutted by technology, their offspring tune in and tune out.

"We live in a time of abundance, and people want to have it all," says Christine Koh. "It's not that parents are doing the wrong things, or doing too much. It's that there's so much available that it can get overwhelming."

In a digital age, "having it all" means many more things than it once did. It means contacting people instantly—and expecting to hear back instantly. Communication is immediate, and immediate gratification can be very addictive. We can DVR a show on TV and access it at any moment. We can download a book to an iPad without ever stepping outside, entering a library, or browsing a bookstore. While there is significant luxury in the technological advances being made, they can pose problems as well.

"No screens," says a professor friend of mine. "There has to be significant time each day where we are not looking at our phone, our computer, the TV. Screens suck us in. We lose ourselves, and that's not good." He insists that his students take notes on paper, and at home he limits his children to one hour of screen time per day. If we can train ourselves to check our e-mail at selected times as opposed to every time our phone makes a noise at us, we are setting a judicious example for our children.

"You're the most important thing right now," our actions tell our children when we leave our phone behind to take a walk with them. "I'm focusing on you." We show them that good manners around technology are not only possible but required. When our daughters are playing on a swing set and hoping we see how high they have managed to go, we miss something—and withhold something from them—if we are buried in our phone, deleting spam or surfing the Internet. The advent of the smartphone becoming "the world in our pocket" is both a blessing and a curse. We must be very conscious of how we use this tool. Anytime we are distracted by it unconsciously, we are telling our children that something behind that screen has priority over them—and we are teaching them to focus on screens themselves.

The other day I was in a grocery store, phone in hand. I was actually looking up a recipe and confirming that the ingredients were in my basket, but to any outer eye, I was checking my e-mail, texting, or tweeting. Focused on the screen of my phone, I was unaware that a woman with a toddler in her arms had come very close to me until I was startled by the shrill scream of her child.

"Phone!" he shrieked. "Give me the phone!"

I jumped back, assuming he was talking to his mother, when I realized that his tiny hand was stretched toward me. He wanted my phone. Badly. As I glanced at his mother for help, I saw that she was busy texting, ignoring the squirming in her arms and the crimson color rising in her son's face.

"Phone!" he wailed at the top of his lungs, and then began a screaming, crying tantrum. His frustrated mother tugged him away, still staring at her phone all the while. The look in her son's eye was crazed, and I saw in that moment the depth of obsession we have with our devices and how, no matter the age, the siren song of the screen is very hard to resist.

Perhaps the crying child learned from his texting mother that a phone, above all else, was his first priority, his ideal companion. And perhaps his obsession was no different from anyone else's—it was simply raw and undisguised in his two-year-old form.

"I allow no video games in the house," says a friend of mine. "And my ten-year-old son is better off for it. Sure, he gets mad and begs. Yes, he plays games sometimes when he visits a friend's house. But I am holding firm. And the fixation always passes. What scares me is seeing parents who indulge their kids with the latest and greatest video games, even playing them with them. They say it's 'a way to spend time together,' but I can't imagine anything more separate. As soon as a kid is playing a video game, it's just him and Mario Kart. There's no one else in the world. It's okay to have fun, but it's a really, really isolating activity."

As parents, we must determine our household rules around these things. Some give a half-hour limit twice a day, maybe an hour twice a day on weekends. Others will let their children play with their phones or iPads when all else fails and they desperately need to occupy their kids in a foolproof—and immediate—way. But for all of us, being thrown back on our own devices—and not the electronic kind—is the more creatively stimulating approach. Technology has its place, but the more of it that is available to us, the more we must be conscious of when and how we use it.

DEVICES OFF
An Exercise

Take one entire evening, and turn off all devices. This includes anything with a screen: cell phones, TVs, computers, iPods. The only rule of the evening is that no screens are viewed. This may cause a great deal of resistance and anxiety, but if you can power through, the connection you will ultimately make with yourself and your family members will be deeper for it.

THE SPRINGBOARD OF
GOOD HEALTH

When we are healthy and active physically, this affects our creative health as well. Nourished and satisfied, our focus improves. Strong and relaxed, we are more secure in our ideas. Physical empowerment helps us take risks in other areas of our lives. The common wish of "health and happiness" is quite literal—the two are often, literally and spiritually, intertwined.

When it comes to our exercise and nutrition habits, two things are guaranteed: our children will notice what we do and they will notice how we feel about what we do. If we are active and we enjoy being active, it is very likely that our children will emulate that. If we are healthy—meaning nutritionally and spiritually healthy—when it comes to choosing our food and activities, our children will learn from that, too.

As a basic rule, the healthiest people practice a healthy moderation with regard to food. No birthday cake? Or a vegan birthday cake? That sounds a bit harsh, especially to my midwestern palate. On the other hand, sugary cereal every day for breakfast? That's probably not a wise choice. The point is that any extreme is likely to be rebelled against, and if we can teach our children a sane and neutral attitude toward food, we will do them well. That being said, we must make our decisions based on the individual reactions and needs of our children. As nutritionist Sara Ryba says, "When it comes to nutritional needs, we are not all created equal." Some people react more or less strongly to sugar, dairy, or wheat. Some people thrive on running, while others need weight training to maintain a physical comfort level. Overall, a gentle balance of healthful foods, the occasional treat, and a cross-training athletic program will suffice for most of us.

We can be inventive as we incorporate healthy habits into our lives, and our children's. Elliot remembers his mother making a canned-pear-half "bunny" for an after-school snack: raisins for eyes, carrot sticks for ears, celery sticks for whiskers, and a small scoop of cottage cheese for a tail. Healthy and fun, it was also quick. It is easy to forget that healthy snacks don't have to take longer to prepare than unhealthy ones. Sometimes unhealthy eating is just a rut we fall into—fast food is cheap and convenient.

Attempting to make healthy habits fun may be just as simple as more consciously using our imaginations. Riding a stick horse is a fun form of exercise, as is playing with the dog or chasing one another around the yard. Participating in physical games with our children sets a great example and provides a chance to bond with one another as well.

But if we are inactive, our children may eventually emulate that, too. Today we may sit at the playground watching them run around. Their weight is fine and they are energetic and strong. We, on the other hand, may be carting around an extra twenty or fifty pounds that we'd rather not be encumbered with. If we do not take care of that, in the long run, our children are more likely than not to imitate what they have seen us do—whether it is late-night bingeing on ice cream or procrastinating doing exercise. And if we have physical problems, chances are that they will develop them as well.

A young mother in my class gained forty pounds when she was pregnant with her twin daughters. Today, her daughters are six and beautiful, and she has gained ten more pounds. "I'm fifty pounds overweight now," she told me. "I know that. I know why, too. I eat the same snacks my daughters eat. I'm tired. I don't exercise. I eat when I can't rest, and I gain weight. Now that it's been six years, I've started to get used to it. I have practically forgotten about my former wardrobe in the back of my closet. I'm used to wearing shapeless things, and I guess if I'm honest, I've sort of given up on myself in that way."

I knew her struggles with weight were painful for her. And for her sake, as much as her daughters', I hoped she would be able to take steps toward a solution that might provide her with some relief. It was, however, her daughter Joanna who performed the necessary intervention.

"We were reading a book about leaders. And then we started talking about leadership," the mother relayed to me the next week at class. "And I asked them who they thought were good leaders, what kinds of leaders they'd like to be. Joanna looked at me, and she said, 'Mommy, you're not a good leader.' I was shocked and hurt and immediately thought of all the things I do for my kids. I love them, I provide for them, I play with them, I encourage them. I asked her why she said that, and she said, 'Because you are always talking about how you have to take better care of yourself and stop eating so much ice cream, but every day you still eat ice cream.'" The young mother's eyes filled with tears of determination. "I joined a weight-loss program that day," she told me. "It's been four days now. I'm still in shock from hearing Joanna's words, and I deserve to be. She called my bluff. Six years old, and she was right."

Her story is not unique. And the good news is that her children will notice what she is doing now, too.

Focusing on positive exploration of what is healthy can be fun for the whole family. "I take my kids to the local farm," says Rob, "and let them pick tomatoes and eat them right there. They love how sweet they are, and they see where fresh vegetables come from. Of course, they love cake and ice cream, too. But it's good to show them that healthy food can also be enjoyable. I just try to strike a balance."

It's fine—even good—to have certain nutrition and exercise

philosophies that you and your family subscribe to. It's just important to be sure that the impulse behind them is coming from a place that is truly healthy in ourselves.

Whether we show our children that we believe our own nutrition and exercise doesn't matter, or if we show them that food is something to be controlled at all costs, we are giving them information that they will absorb and repurpose. Extreme regimens of any kind, when treated as if they are the only answer and imposed on others, are to be avoided. It may be fine for a grown adult to experiment with radical diets, but imposing them on everyone else can be off-putting, hindering the health and happiness of others.

"I think that parents try to push on their kids what they feel they lack themselves—or, in other words, try to make their kids a more perfect version of themselves," says Lee, a student in my Santa Fe class, "and it's dangerous. If they are heavy, they may push their kids not to be. Or if they're losing weight, they may push their kids to lose weight, too." Of course, there is a healthy balance to everything, and in an ideal world, we all would be at a reasonable weight. But when things start to go to the extreme—be it eating fast food every day or eating only lettuce—we do a disservice to ourselves and our children. By becoming aware of our own nutrition and exercise habits, we become aware of what we are passing on to our children.

Children learn by what we do. If we want active, healthy children, we must be active and healthy ourselves. We can exercise and invite our children to exercise with us. Sometimes it's a trip to the park, sometimes it's a walk, sometimes it's calisthenics right on the living room floor. The important point is that our children see we are enjoying our bodies. When Domenica was little and we lived in Greenwich Village, I got exercise for both of us by mounting Domenica on a stick horse and trotting her to and from school. I taught her "whoa" for red lights and "giddy up" for green. She had several stick horses from which to choose. Her favorite—and the fastest—was a golden palomino. On days when she rode Goldie, our exercise was a little more strenuous. She would gallop, not just trot. I hastened to keep up with her. At the school's door, she relinquished her mount. I would lead her pony back home. From nine-thirty to two-thirty I had writing time. Then it was time to select a stick horse for Domenica to ride back home. My favorite was a bay with a snow-white blaze. Sometimes Domenica would object that she rode to school on one pony and went home on another. But we would trot briskly home, no matter which mount I'd selected. Making a game of the walk, we incorporated activity into every day without strain. Small, healthy actions, with the intention of play and joy within them, can add up to a healthy life.

BABY STEPS

An Exercise

What steps can you take to improve your own health and nutrition? Allow yourself to take pen in hand and muse on the page for a few minutes. Although this can feel overwhelming for many of us, remember that small steps forward on your part make a large impact on your quality of life—and on your children.

THE DREAMINESS OF SLEEP

Today in my Morning Pages, I found myself writing: "I didn't sleep well last night. I am tired and wired." And tired and wired is exactly what we all become when we are overtaxed and under-rested. Sleep deprivation prevents our children from having the focus to play and create productively. And we are not the most supportive parents when we are crabby and exhausted. For ourselves and our kids, we must do our best to value sleep and the restful rituals we can build to enhance it.

There are volumes of research on the benefits of sleep for children: they're healthier, more even-tempered, better students. Our home lives confirm this—we know what happens when we don't get enough sleep or when our children don't. Tempers rise and patience lags. Focus suffers, and we make more mistakes. Our children resist the things they usually love, and when we suggest that they're "just tired," anger flares. "No, I'm *not*," they respond defiantly.

Looking at this, we see how we, too, may suffer from the same denial. We decide we can't get any more sleep than we have, and that we're "just fine." We then proceed to force ourselves through our day with the hope that it won't matter. But it does matter. Taking moments to rest when we can, taking naps when our children do (if we can), and modeling good sleep and rest habits allow us to communicate this value to our children. If our children don't want to lie down for their naps, we tell them they have to lie down anyway. Soon they are sound asleep, and it's hard to believe that, just moments before, they had resisted the idea so completely. Pushing through our own fatigue, we can learn from our children. We, too, are resisting our naps. We believe there are other things more important for us to do. But resting ourselves makes us more available, more patient, more alert.

Often, parents are so exhausted that they can't imagine ever catching up. Sleep deprivation builds over time, and it also takes time to correct. "I'm asleep in a second," says Nancy, a new mom. "I close my eyes and I'm gone. I can't imagine not being tired." For Nancy, there is a level at which the reality of her current situation—two to three middle-of-the-night feedings—will keep her from getting enough sleep. But it is worth it for her to take whatever moments she can and allow herself to rest. She won't be able to catch up in one fell swoop. But valuing sleep as a high priority for herself, even amid the many other things she needs to do, will help her be more efficient in all areas of her life and parenting.

For our children, we can encourage restfulness by taking as many steps as we can to make their bedrooms serene. Having them clean up their rooms, however much they may resist it, does create a calmer environment more conducive to sleep. Controlling the amount of light and noise as they are falling asleep is comforting as they drift off. Many times, the hardest part is pulling them away from whatever they are doing to begin the evening bath-and-bed routine. But if there can be some fun woven in—toys in the bath, a book before bed—this ritual, too, can be enjoyable, and everyone will be healthier for it.

BUILDING A CALM ENVIRONMENT
An Exercise

Often a few very small changes will make our sleeping environment a more restful place. Simply dusting the headboard and clearing the nightstands can add a great dose of serenity to our own sleeping area. For our children, a calming night light or gentle fan can add an element of comfort as they unwind.

Find one small change you can make in your own sleeping area and one small change you can make in your child's. Do you notice a difference as you begin bedtime routines?

RITUAL

Casting my mind back over my own private memories, I find that those I cherish most involve ritual. There was the nightly reading of a bedtime story, sometimes a new book from the library, sometimes a cherished favorite we had read many times before. What mattered was the consistency—knowing that I could count on a story to give closure to the day. Children thrive on consistency. This means, in other words, that they thrive on ritual.

Many rituals can be built into your child's day. There is the ritual of grace before meals. There is the ritual of the nightly bath, the ritual of putting on pajamas and saying bedtime prayers before lights out. Know that your child takes comfort from them all. The reading ritual might begin each night with the signature phrase

"Once upon a time . . ." In the Cameron home, the nightly prayer would be the classic "Now I lay me down to sleep . . ." For the bath, I remember the beloved doggerel "Rub-a-dub-dub, three men in the tub." At mealtime, we always said grace before we ate. In all homes, rituals can be customized. And in all rituals, it is the thought that counts. We are teaching our children to appreciate the gifts of their life.

Mary Lou, a single mother, found that creating ritual created ease for herself. Her young daughter became used to the rhythm of evening activities, and they both were calmer for it. Homework, Dinner, Reading, Bath, Bedtime. Mary Lou added proactive steps to their rituals as well: As soon as homework was done, it was put carefully into her daughter's backpack, which waited in its place by the door. After dinner, Mary Lou spent a few minutes cleaning the kitchen and set the table for breakfast. At bathtime, clothes were sorted into laundry baskets, "dark, light, colors," and the outfit for tomorrow was laid out on a chair. A quick check-in with the highlight of the day, and the stress of a long day was laid to rest at bedtime with the simple prayer that Mary Lou concocted herself: "Now I lay me down to sleep, I pray the Lord my soul to keep. And if I dream before I wake, I pray good dreams the Lord will make." Mary Lou and her daughter recited "their" prayer together nightly, and turned in. Prepared for the day to come, they both rested better at night. And, when morning came, there was no mad dash to choose an outfit or collect homework before the school bus came. They both had time for a non-rushed breakfast and quick check-in before their respective days began.

A ritual is not only a repeated act but a momentary pause, a conscious, reflective break. Building ritual into a child's day, we teach the child the importance of rest. So much of modern life goes pell-mell. Learning to pause and count our blessings is an invaluable skill.

Morning Pages can become a valuable and familiar ritual that connects us to ourselves and our day. They clear our consciousness, like the windshield wipers swiping across the windshield of our psyches. I know mothers of infants who rock their children in one arm while writing with the other. I know parents of six-year-olds who encourage their children to write first thing in the morning as well. It can become a family ritual to have daily, reflective time every morning.

In the evening, the practice of Highlights brings not only a sense of stability and safety but also one of connection and optimism. This trained optimism, choosing the highest point of the day and sharing it with a loved one, gives us a gift of gratitude that we carry through our lives. Highlights—ours and our children's—often surprise us. Recently a young father I know had a long-awaited opening night for a play he had written. "It was years in the making," he said. "I spent every day of my life thinking about that play as it came to fruition. And the day it opened, it wasn't the good reviews or the fancy guests that made my Highlights list. All of those things were so exciting. But when I shared Highlights that night with my son, I realized the highlight of my day was that I was able to show my son that if you reach for a goal—even a very ambitious one, like writing and producing a play—you can achieve it. I was setting a good example for my son that day."

It is not uncommon for Highlights to surprise us. As in all ritual, it is not the size of the action that matters. It is the thoughtfulness and regularity that makes an impact. In small-town Vermont, Alisa walked each day to school with her best friend. She would leave her house at exactly 8:00 a.m. and meet her friend Amy at 8:05 on Amy's porch. Together they would walk to school, easily arriving before 8:20, when they were due. They walked together from third grade on, crossing the street with the same crossing guard every morning and on the return trip home. They shared stories from home and from school, of homework and siblings and pets, of new toys and longed-for toys. They sometimes walked in silence. And by the time they were in high school, they were still best friends. "That's a connection we'll always have," says Alisa. When she and Amy see each other now, as adults, they always take a walk together. That familiar ritual of walking and talking is one that still brings comfort to both of them.

The larger events of the year, too, gift us with opportunities for ritual. Birthdays promise cake with candles to blow out. "You matter," we tell our children when we let them choose the menu or the restaurant for their birthday dinner. "I'm glad you were born and I celebrate your special day," we are saying when we hand them a wrapped birthday gift. Whether it's an annual holiday celebration or a weekly Sunday-morning pancake breakfast, we gift our children with safety when we practice ritual. "We are building a life together," our actions tell them. "We are making things together that bring us happiness."

Ritual provides joyful structure, a break within our day that puts us in touch with ourselves. As we commit to Morning Pages, we bring ourselves a time of reflection and peace that we carry with us throughout our day. As we build ritual, large and small, into our children's lives, we create a foundation of security and whimsy that becomes a part of how they, too, learn to exist in the world with confidence and faith.

RETURNING TO RITUAL
An Exercise

What rituals from your own childhood do you remember the most fondly?

What small ritual could you create with your children today? Could you bring one of your cherished childhood experiences into your child's life, carrying on the tradition?

Chapter Nine

CULTIVATING DISCOVERY

~

We teach our children to be brave through our own bravery, honest by our own honesty. As we are willing to be beginners, we model for our children the grace of starting something new. Setting aside perfectionism, we embrace process over product. Valuing ourselves and our endeavors, we learn a healthy immunity to criticism. Our children do the same. As our children enter school and participate in new and different activities, we work to encourage and maintain their optimism and willingness to try new things. We take every action we can to ensure our children's safety, creative and otherwise, and with our knowledge of the potential pitfalls comes responsibility. But our understanding grants us power, and we can consciously protect and guide our children as they discover their own creative identities.

PERFECT ENOUGH

Children learn by what we do. If we allow ourselves to create freely, without the need for perfection, our children learn to do likewise. When Domenica was little, I often entertained her by drawing horses and dogs. My horses looked real enough, but my dogs? My dogs had an alarming tendency to look like cats.

"Draw Calla Lily," Domenica would demand, naming our white standard poodle. "That *is* Calla Lily," I would defend myself.

"The ears are wrong," Domenica would say.

"They're okay," I would defend myself.

"Try again," Domenica would command.

And so I would try again, rendering a dog that was slightly more doglike.

"Now you try it," I would urge her. And try she did, drawing a dog that looked more doglike than mine, but still imperfect.

"Bravo!" I would applaud her. "That's excellent," I would say.

"It's not right," Domenica would protest.

"It's really very good," I would say.

Domenica's horses, like mine, were more horselike.

"Oh, that's very good," I would praise her.

As Domenica grew older, her drawings grew more and more accurate, but her standards also rose.

"Draw me Silver Lily," I would say, naming her childhood pony, and a creditable Silver Lily would emerge. Still, the rendering was not quite perfect, and she was frustrated by that. "It's still very good," I would tell her. "It's good enough."

Working in clay, Domenica managed to create horselike figures. They weren't perfect, but they were, I told her, "perfect enough."

When Domenica was in fifth grade, she received a daunting assignment: write a story and illustrate it. Her story, predictably, involved horses, and her illustrations were decent renderings of the horses she described. I still have Domenica's "book." It wasn't perfect, just perfect enough.

As parents, we have a responsibility to model imperfection, especially if we are adept in an area that interests our child. An actor friend of mine shows her budding actress daughter films of her earliest monologue rehearsals and of herself in her school play. "See? Everyone starts as a beginner," she tells her daughter. The path to mastery is a long one, no matter the natural talent. It falls to us to show this to our children and to let them see the ups and downs of our own journey, our own imperfect process.

Modeling imperfection also models the faith to try again, to begin anew. In every creative life there are setbacks, and the successful people are not the ones who never fail but the ones who get up and try again after their failures. The faster we can get up, the better. Wallowing in our mistakes only reinforces the behavior of wallowing in our mistakes. Correcting our mistakes, on the other hand, being willing to move forward and willing to make more mistakes, embraces that making—and learning from—our mistakes is an inevitable part of moving ahead.

Our children are exposed to extreme accomplishment on a daily basis, whether it is watching child prodigies or young athletes on TV or YouTube. Because the extraordinary is so easily accessible, children are inundated with images of finished products without any discussion or documentation of the years of blood, sweat, and tears that went into producing their now-flawless performances. Amateurism—which translates to "for love"—is a wonderful goal as we urge our children not to be perfect, but to explore creative outlets for pleasure and for pleasure alone, without the pressure of someone else's "perfect" performance as the only worthy goal.

Perfection is, first and foremost, an unattainable mirage. It will always hover out of reach. Perfectionism is a blocking device. It is a refusal to move ahead. It is a debilitating loop that causes us to lose sight of the larger picture as we become obsessed with the details. Instead of creating freely, experimenting, and allowing misguided choices to reveal themselves later, we drive ourselves crazy trying to get every detail right before we put our pen to the paper or the horn to our lips. We "correct" ourselves to the point where our creative act becomes bland and joyless, where our original spark of inspiration is in danger of being smothered.

Artists who create freely and correct later are productive. They are happy. And they are the people who have a body of work to show for their efforts. When we erase until the paper tears, or see our children doing this, we must halt the obsession. Perfectionism is not a quest for the best—it is the pursuit of the worst in ourselves, the part that tells us we will never be good enough. Perfection is egotism parading as virtue. Do not be fooled. We are good enough. And our children are good enough, as well.

MODELING IMPERFECTION
An Exercise

Fill in the following blanks:

If I didn't have to do it perfectly, I would try

_____.

If I didn't have to do it perfectly, I would try

_____.

If I didn't have to do it perfectly, I would try

_____.

If I didn't have to do it perfectly, I would try

_____.

If I didn't have to do it perfectly, I would try

_____.

Try modeling imperfection for your child. Choose something you know you will not do perfectly and allow your child to witness this.

Now ask your child, if she could try any creative activity that she's never tried before, what would it be? See if you can devise a way for her to take a small step into the realm she mentions. It does not have to be large. If she says "cowgirl," perhaps there is a horse ranch nearby where she could pet a velvety nose. If she says "moviemaker," allow her to film a short movie on your phone or camera. Allow yourself—and your child—to be imperfect as you work with this exercise. You are after fun, not finesse.

HONESTY

Morning Pages help us detach from our censor and allow us a place to vent, celebrate, wonder, dream, plan. Since there is no wrong way to do Morning Pages, we can allow ourselves complete freedom within their confines. Doing Morning Pages, we enter the world more clearheaded. Doing Morning Pages for an extended period of time, we begin to speak up where we may have remained silent in the past.

"That's okay," we may have trained ourselves to respond when the plumber was an hour late, when the babysitter canceled, when our children refused to eat what we'd cooked even after an hour of coaxing. "It's not the end of the world," we decided, and we were probably right about that. But what do we really mean when we say, "That's okay"? Do we actually feel "okay," or do we really feel frustrated, inconvenienced, invisible, disrespected, dispassionate, accepting? "Okay" covers a gamut of emotions, and as we work with Morning Pages, we find ourselves being more specific and more honest about what we actually feel.

"Actually, I can't afford for you to be late today," we tell the plumber. "I will go ahead and call someone else if you aren't able to arrive at the time we planned." As we experiment with voicing our feelings honestly, we discover our boundaries. We come to clarity.

Many of us harbor a belief that we must sacrifice our selves for our children. This is misplaced martyrdom. Our children do better when we are authentically ourselves. When Domenica was still young enough to be playpen-bound, I would place her amid a tower of toys and sit down to write. I would cue up nursery rhymes, feeling martyred as I tried for endless patience. Finally, one day I couldn't take it any longer. I cued up the Rolling Stones song "Brown Sugar."

"This is what your mommy really likes," I told Domenica, who teetered on wobbly legs, dancing to the beat. From that day onward, I played music I liked, and Domenica responded with lively enthusiasm. I played Bruce Springsteen and told her, "Mommy likes 'Thunder Road.'" To my delight, Domenica also responded to this anthem. She gurgled with glee. "Like it!" she called out, dancing happily.

There is a great relief in allowing ourselves to be honest. There is a great relief in admitting our true feelings. As we begin to trust ourselves, showing ourselves that we care what we are feeling, that we are listening, we are able to express ourselves appropriately and kindly. It is when we try to stuff our complex emotions into "It's okay" that we risk exploding and losing control of what comes out of our mouths. When we express our emotions honestly, we give our children permission to do the same.

As our children grow, they also start to identify and voice their own boundaries and opinions. As they do, we must turn a tuned ear toward what they are saying. Yes, it may be quite inconvenient when they announce that they are not going to eat broccoli or when they tear up the book we have just bought. But rebelliousness is a sign of growing independence, and just as we do not want to live a life where we stuff our feelings, our children also desire to express their newly developing attitudes and opinions. Recognizing this, we learn to practice compassion.

Observing our children and giving them room to express themselves, we see the snowflake pattern of their souls beginning to reveal itself. This is not to say that the growth process should just be a free-for-all where we relinquish control altogether. Rather, by setting clear boundaries and structures within which our children can be free to express themselves, we give them true safety: the encouragement to make their own discoveries and the room in which to do it.

HONEST FEELINGS
An Exercise

Fill in the blanks quickly:

If I let myself admit it, I feel _____.
If I let myself admit it, I feel _____.
If I let myself admit it, I feel _____.
If I let myself admit it, I feel _____.
If I let myself admit it, I feel _____.

EDUCATION

"Creativity is more than giving your kids paints and paper," says Russell Granet, a leading expert in arts education. "It's a way to see the world, a way to look at things." Granet is the founder of the Arts Education Resource in New York City and the executive director of the Lincoln Center Institute. He argues that quality arts education is a right, not a privilege, for all learners. His impact on the field has been far-reaching and impressive, and as an academic, artist, teacher, and father, his passion for the arts is palpable and definitive.

"If we go through the world looking through the lens of creativity, we set up innovative thinking in our kids. I think that non-artists should actively think like artists. That creative problem-solving skill is transferrable, and we have to teach our kids that." Granet acknowledges the pressures of being a parent, navigating school, play, and home routines. "The rituals and realities of parenthood exist," he affirms, "and we have to be creative within them. We have to make dinner. We have to prepare the bath and help our kids do homework. But we can indulge a stream of artistic consciousness along the way. Art is a springboard for everything else."

When I ask Granet what he thinks most hinders our children in the educational realm, he answers me without hesitation. "Test pressure," he says. "There's pressure on the kid, the parent, the teacher, the principal to deliver high test scores. At about age seven, the pressure to perform on tests begins."

As long as there is pressure to test well, there is pressure on getting the "right" answer. "Learning becomes about right versus wrong, and the stakes are very high to be right," Granet says. Where is there room for creative thinking, and where is there room for kids to make mistakes? Mistakes are valuable. We learn from mistakes. And if we are learning only that we'd better not make any mistakes, we are in a precarious position indeed.

"In school, kids are put into categories: creative or intelligent," Granet continues. "This ignores crossover and does a disservice to the kids. It perpetuates the myth that there is no crossover. And as long as we perpetuate that myth, we perpetuate that reality."

If schools do not, in general, foster creativity, then the responsibility falls on the parent to find these opportunities. If art classes are not offered at our children's schools, then we must find or create opportunities for our children to explore the arts.

Nancy, a mom of two in Indianapolis, puts it this way: "Parents have to take their kids' creative education into their own hands. Yes, there's cost involved. But if we can put our kids in sports, we can take them to a community theater play. We can expose them to the arts, whether they think they're going to like it or not. If we don't show them what's out there, and they're not getting it at school, then how will they ever know their own possibility?"

With pressure to perform in school and "right" answers threatening to matter above all else, it is all the more important that we shepherd our children toward creativity. Judging early artistic efforts is artist abuse. Ridiculing interests or attempts is cruel. We also must be on the lookout for those who would undermine our children's nascent creative impulses. We cannot tolerate anyone who throws this kind of cold water on the burgeoning creativity of our child. As much as we can, we must model a healthy respect for this exploration and let our children know that not only are their creative impulses fun, they are vital.

In an overscheduled, high-intensity academic culture, children are sleep-deprived and overwhelmed with homework at a frighteningly young age. Pressured to do more so that their chances of getting into college are increased, they are at risk of adding activities that are not of their own choosing, activities about which they are not truly passionate. Pushing themselves to excel for the sake of excelling, they are unlikely to gain pleasure from the act of learning—or retain much information past the test date. They count the minutes until "the job is done" and learn that they must work, satisfied or not, for the sake of work rather than follow a passion that may, indeed, lead to a great deal of satisfying work.

"The saddest thing I've seen," says Christine Koh, "is creativity take a backseat to academics." When students are scolded for their creative "wrong" answers, they are taught to not create. They are taught to stuff their imagination and focus on rote. The academic shaming that exists in our culture is both rampant and tragic.

It took years of teaching in academia, a dubious privilege that I myself experienced, to identify the elusive but deadly enmity that academia harbors toward creativity. Outright hostility is one thing. It can be encountered and responded to. But infinitely more deadly and terrifying is the subtle discounting that may numb student creativity in the academic setting.

Student work, when scrutinized, is seldom appreciated. It is a rare teacher who will acknowledge strengths as often and as readily as he or she points out shortcomings. I am not arguing that the world of academia should become an exalted artists' studio. It is, however, my point that creative, intuitive little souls who are trying to flourish and grow become crippled when they are forced to become overly cerebral. When youngsters are daunted early and unfairly because of their inability to conform to a norm that is not their own, a long road to creative recovery is paved ahead of them. Without specific tools, ego strength, or language, many creatives who are routinely squelched in academic settings languish for years in the wake of these shaming experiences.

Sometimes, opportunity will knock for our children. We are faced, then, with a decision. Do we allow them to move forward in an audition process that could take them out of school and onto a national stage—or lead to heartrending rejection? If they are selected to be in a television commercial, do the proceeds from that commercial go into a bank account that is theirs to access at a later date or to a college fund? In these rare and extreme cases, we must judge our children's needs and desires on an individual basis. There are stories of young working artists that end well, and then there are those that do not. As long as we encourage and support our children's individual voices as we navigate the process, the odds are in our favor.

When Audrey was in second grade, she took a standardized test to determine placement in elementary school. Placing in the top percentile and labeled "highly creative," she was invited to attend a small magnet elementary school. It would mean leaving her circle of friends and the known world she had experienced to date. But Audrey had not enjoyed second grade. She had often been singled out for not conforming, and after much discussion, her parents decided to enroll her in the magnet school, where she would know no one, but where perhaps her own individuality would be encouraged more than before.

"It was here that, for the first time, I had teachers who embraced me and all of my idiosyncrasies," Audrey recalls. "The projects and assignments were graded on both academic performance and creativity. Here, I was the 'theater kid' and the 'funny one' instead of a 'smart aleck,' as I had been described in my old school, where my teachers seemed to spend every day trying to stamp out my creative impulses. Going to Magnet gave me the confidence to continue down that path of self-expression and exploration through middle school and beyond." It is interesting to note that Audrey, and an impossibly high percentage of her classmates at Magnet, are now professionally successful in some area of the arts. All of them credit their elementary school with their later success.

"I wasn't sure if the new school would be a legitimate opportunity, or if it might be suffocating for her—too much, too soon of everything," Audrey's mother remembers now. "I like to keep a balance with my kids. But she wasn't finding what she needed in her school. And happily, she did find it at Magnet. I'm glad I let her go."

Allowing our children to blossom creatively does not mean that they will become professional artists, but it does mean that they are more likely to enter a profession where they are more fully themselves.

With active parents who are aware of what their children must find outside of their school, there is hope for our children's creative blossoming. And with educators such as Russell Granet at the forefront of the field, there is hope for the educational system as well. By focusing on what we can do as parents, we can counter a misguided educational system.

FROM CHILD TO PARENT
An Exercise

Choose something that your child knows more about than you do, and ask him to give you a lesson in it. Be open to learning and open to his knowledge. His own act of teaching—and your enthusiastic learning—is likely to thrill him. "You know things," this tells him. "You have something to say, something to teach. I want to learn from you."

THE MONSTER IN THE CLOSET:
SHAME AND CRITICISM

When our children cry out in the night, afraid that there's something in the closet or under the bed, we confidently tell them that there's nothing to be afraid of. We're right next door, their teddy bear is here to protect them, and everything is going to be okay. "It's not real," we tell them. "You're safe."

When our children are unfairly shamed or criticized, however, sometimes by our own words, assisting in their recovery will require some finesse on our part. Shaming our children for their artistic expression is something we must be careful to avoid. If we do find ourselves lashing out, we must be quick to make amends. "Stop singing! You're really annoying me!" may require an addendum: "I want you to sing and express yourself. You have a beautiful voice. I was just frustrated because it was getting very loud and I couldn't hear Aunt Cynthia on the phone."

Looking back at our own histories, were there times when we were made to feel foolish for wanting to express ourselves? We must be aware that our own unmourned losses create emotional scar tissue, and in an effort to avoid our own wounds, we may push our children's early artistic attempts away.

"My mother was beautiful," says Holly. "She was a southern woman, tall, thin, and gorgeous. She prided herself on her manners, style, and decorum, and wanted her daughters to emulate the same." Holly's two older sisters were the spitting image of their mother: stunning brunettes with slight frames. But Holly was very different. Nearly a foot shorter, with a stocky build and dirty-blond hair, Holly had her father's athletic physique.

"I wasn't like my sisters, and I was always aware of that," she remembers now. "They took ballet from age five, and I tried to follow in their footsteps, but I was about as far from a natural ballerina as you could get. I switched to gymnastics," says Holly, "and I became a great tumbler—a power gymnast. By age ten I was competing in junior events. And by age ten, I was aware that my short, muscular build might be okay in the gym, but it didn't look right in the dresses my mother wanted me to wear for the parties she threw. So I started making my own clothes. I loved expressing myself that way, and even though my mother didn't approve of the crazy designs and combinations I came up with, I made them—and wore them—anyway. She didn't like it, but in general, she didn't stop me."

Holly remembers one particularly painful day. "My aunt and cousins came for a dinner party. I was eleven, and I had just won the highest award I'd ever won in gymnastics. I had the ribbon in my bedroom and I could hardly wait to share it. I put together another one of my crazy outfits, and came downstairs proud of what I was wearing. My mother was horrified, saying that I couldn't 'wear that for company.' She forced me into the same dress my sisters were wearing and I was uncomfortable and out of place strapped inside its pink frills. Trying to improve how I looked, I added some bracelets I had made and pulled my hair into a long, sideways braid. When my aunt and cousins arrived, we stood on the porch waiting to greet them. My aunt looked us all up and down, and then turned to my mother. 'Well, at least two of them got your looks and sense of style,' she said. I was totally embarrassed. I didn't say a word the whole night, and I didn't show my gymnastics ribbon to anyone."

Now Holly looks back on pictures of herself at that time. "I looked great," she says ruefully. "I looked athletic and strong. But I felt nothing but awkward compared to my mother and sisters and their southern ideal of beauty. When I see pictures of myself wearing what I wanted to wear, I see a real personality. But it wasn't mirrored back to me as something good, and it made me feel embarrassed of myself as a person, and diminished the value of my being an athlete. I wish I could go back and reassure that kid."

Holly's story is one that is, sadly, common. Made to feel physically awkward, we recoil from the spotlight. The athlete who may shine on the gymnastics mat, hamming it up for the judges, shrinks from sight in an ill-fitting dress that is asking her to be someone she's not. Asked to be someone she's not, it's a short trip to starting to doubt herself as a gymnast as well. Shamed for her different build as well as for her creative attempts at dressing herself, Holly was doubly stung. "I wanted to be invisible that night," she remembers. "That was all I wanted."

Being shamed for expressing ourselves or being criticized unfairly, we start to learn that putting any expression out into the world for attention is a dangerous act. Being wrongly shamed as creatives, we learn that we are wrong to create. Burying this belief under apathy or pessimism, the shame lives on, doing push-ups while it waits for us to try expressing ourselves again, only to resurface stronger than ever.

This is why many of us feel embarrassed to admit our own creative dreams. This is why many of us are afraid of the creative dreams emerging in our children.

We must, must be brave here. We must face the things that we do not want to face in ourselves, or we risk remaining blocked and discouraging our children as well. Am I saying that there is no such thing as helpful criticism? Of course not. Intelligent criticism, insight that gives us an internal *aha!* and lights the way forward in a gentle, productive way is right criticism. Criticism that shames, that asks "How dare you?," that snickers, that nitpicks, is wrong criticism. Shame is a controlling device. Shaming someone is an attempt to avoid our own shame. Shaming someone else is an attempt to prevent another person from acting in a way that will trigger our own embarrassments.

The act of making art is both scary and healing. Art brings light to places that have remained dark. Art brings perspective. Making art, at any level, is an act of courage and an expression of faith.

When our children are shamed or criticized, we must be very firm in our support: do not pick up the first doubt. We cannot allow negative thinking to take hold. We must protect ourselves and our children as much as we can from useless criticism. It is impossible to avoid it completely, and so, when wrong criticism arrives on your doorstep, there are a few steps you must take:

- Do something very nurturing. Treat the recipient of the criticism with a concrete action of kindness.
- Look closely at the criticism. What does it remind you of? What does it say about the critic? Criticism is as relevant to—if not more relevant to—the giver than the recipient.
- Make something with your child. If a painting has been criticized for being too "crazy," paint something even crazier.

Creativity is the only cure for criticism.

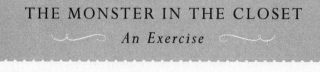

THE MONSTER IN THE CLOSET
An Exercise

Fill in the blanks quickly. Do not overthink this exercise.

I felt shamed when _____.

One person who shamed me was _____.

When I felt shamed, I decided that _____.

When I try to shame someone else, I suspect
   that it is because _____.

One kind and healing thing I could do
   for myself is _____.

One kind and healing thing I could do
   for my child is _____.

Chapter Ten

CULTIVATING HUMILITY

~

In making artful lives, we learn to be right-sized. Practicing modesty, we learn humility. Our children, too, become right-sized as they measure their endeavors against their own standards, not those of others. We are correct to actively appreciate our children's gifts, but acknowledging their creative lives and the accomplishments of their siblings and peers is a delicate issue. Even with the best of intentions, overemphasizing our children's achievements can foster perfectionism, competitiveness, and disconnection from God's plan. Humble, we are all at our most empowered. Humble, we are closest to God.

THE FAME DRUG

Ah, fame. It is an American drug, a poisonous, rampant distraction. It attacks us at every age, telling us that if it hasn't happened yet, it's not going to happen. (Translation: It's too late. You're not good enough. Why even try?) We watch the news and see headlines in newspapers of enormous success by people (1) younger than we or our children are; (2) less talented, in our eyes, than we or our children are; (3) richer and more glamorous than we are.

As soon as we start comparing ourselves with a Hollywood norm, we are talking ourselves out of taking action. "I can't catch up with that," we think, "so why even try to do anything?" Or, "That's totally unfair. Her daughter is not as talented as mine, but her family is rich because of the opportunity her daughter was given." It is a short road from these thoughts to "What's the use?" And as soon as we are thinking "What's the use?" we are dangerously close to rationalizing ourselves out of making any effort at all.

This morning a friend of mine called. She is mid-divorce and soon to be a single parent to her only son. She is rightfully scared, and, to my ear, trying to focus on anything but the uncomfortable day-to-day requirements of her current situation.

"I need to write a book," she tells me. "Or a screenplay. But it has to be a hit, and then I'll be rich and famous and I won't have to worry about anything."

Hmm, I think. "I have to write a hit" is a slippery place to begin. "I have to write what I have to write" is where we have more secure footing. Maybe my friend will write a hit book or screenplay. But with this as the starting goal for her first writing endeavor, she is setting the bar unnecessarily high for herself. Does she want to write? Does she feel called to write and to express herself? Or does she want to be rich and famous so she "won't have to worry about anything"? Perhaps what she really desires is a break from worry.

Earning money and gaining acclaim for our creative endeavors rarely gives us a break. More often, the opposite occurs. We are more in demand. There is more pressure. There are more requests, more people asking us for, well, *more*. "Fame is a by-product," my literary agent friend says. "People are constantly asking me to 'make them famous.' Fame comes, once in a while, from doing the work. It can't be the goal, and it's the part of the equation we have the least power over. My job is to help artists do good work and be compensated fairly for that work," she says. "Anyone who claims to be a star-maker is focusing on the wrong things and, frankly, making an empty promise."

Fame exists at every level. It may be on the national or international stage, or it may be a perceived hierarchy within our small community. Focusing on fame interferes with what we are doing, and with what our children are doing. Instead of being proud of your daughter for being in the school play, you become obsessed with how she was partly cut off in the picture in the local newspaper, or how another girl got the attention that your daughter deserved. The goal becomes being recognized for being in a play instead of enjoying the process of being in a play.

By rewarding effort, praising process more than product, we instill in our children a desire to fulfill their own potential. No matter someone's level of natural ability; to achieve great things, every person must put forth great effort. As Thomas Alva Edison put it, "Genius is one percent inspiration, ninety-nine percent perspiration." As long as our children know that the work is never done, the depth of their potential is limitless.

It is more effective to reward daily piano practice than to overly celebrate the "win" at a local piano contest. Excellence is wonderful, but there is always another, larger contest. "Winning" is temporary and must be put in perspective as a joyful occasion, but not an end in and of itself. Growth occurs in spurts and is an erratic forward movement: two steps forward, one step back. With ourselves and our children, we must be gentle. In the daily, conscious effort forward lies the magic of potential and the true power of action.

All of us like—and deserve—to be acknowledged for our efforts. We can't guarantee that we will be acknowledged exactly when and how we want to be acknowledged. But we will never be satisfied as long as we are obsessed with outer praise for our actions. When we focus outside ourselves and compare ourselves with others who make us feel that we are coming up short, we are always focusing on lack. When we focus on lack, our joy in the process starts to wither. When we focus on lack, we discredit ourselves and lessen our excitement for the well-earned accomplishments of others. Fame is fickle, and fame can be toxic.

At every level, on any topic, the fame drug can disable us. A student in my class talks of her recent experience during the summer break.

"The other day I was at the pool with my kids. A bunch of moms were there, and I listened to them gossip about the rankings everyone had gotten at last week's swim meet. I heard them whispering about one kid who won almost every blue ribbon. 'His mom's over there,' a woman snipped, 'probably trying to see if she can get his picture in the newspaper again.' I looked over at the mom, and she wasn't doing anything. Her son had beaten the other kids fair and square. I said as much and I wasn't popular for it, but I'll tell you, it got a lot quieter on our side of the pool. I'd rather hear an awkward silence than hear some mom complaining about another kid's unfair advantage. All of our kids swim. All of our kids get ribbons sometimes. It's just not the end of the world. I don't want to become an ugly person because of the color of a ribbon."

Focusing on generosity toward and encouragement of ourselves and others, we become strong. Allowing our children to know that we see and enjoy their efforts, they are seen and enjoyed. Small, concrete actions on behalf of ourselves and on behalf of our children lessen fame's grip on our soul. When your daughter is in the school play, you can celebrate this by making a scrapbook of memories with her. We can save the ticket stub and a piece of fabric from her costume. We can help her rehearse her lines and clap from the audience. We can videotape the performance and send it to grandparents and friends. And when the play is over, we can ask her what she would like to do next.

THE WISH LIST
An Exercise

When we are seized by the fame drug, we are focused on someone else. To break this painful obsession, we must turn our focus to ourselves. In this moment, we do well to quickly get in touch with our own true desires. The fame drug encourages us to be consumed with something outside of ourselves, something of which we will never get "enough." But our true power lies in being focused within rather than without. One of the fastest ways I know to change our focus back onto our authentic selves is with a tool called "the wish list." The wish list is deceptively simple—simply complete the sentence "I wish . . ." twenty-five times.

Examples:

I wish I had time to get a massage.
I wish I could lose ten pounds.
I wish I had clarity about Jeff and could move on,
    unconfused about that relationship.
I wish I'd take the time to really scrub the terrace.
I wish I could afford to buy a new car.

Try it now. Your wishes may be large or small, sublime or ridiculous. There is no wrong wish.

I wish _____.

When I use this tool, and when my students use this tool, a certain magic is unlocked. We cast our imaginations into the future and picture our desires as having come true. For a moment, we pretend that we have what we wish for. In that moment, we contact both our desire and the possibility of that desire being fulfilled.

Making these lists, we become in touch with ourselves. Because there is no wrong wish, our ideas are free to come to us, unconstrained. It is a powerful tool, and I urge my students to write their wishes down often—and save those lists. It is very common to return to the list weeks or months later and see that, indeed, many of those wishes have been "granted."

COMPETITION

Competition, like the numbing haze of fame, is a spiritual drug. Competition compares our "insides" with someone else's "outsides." Competition focuses on winning and losing, succeeding and failing, rather than on the task at hand: are we doing our personal best? Are we taking the steps we know are necessary to take? Are we enjoying our endeavor? When we take our focus off ourselves and place it squarely on someone else—the competition—we block our own good and impede our own progress.

It is a paradox that those who are not focused on others usually make the swiftest progress and easily hold their lead. When we focus on ourselves and our own next right step, we are satisfied. We are moving at our own right pace, and we are fulfilled by the journey.

When we fall under the spell of competition and focus on someone else's progress instead of our own, we are indulging in the myth that it is one or the other—either his child will succeed or my child will succeed. Either I am the better mother or she is the better mother. We must be careful to create an environment where there's plenty of praise to go around. As we show our children that we appreciate their efforts as well as compliment the efforts of their peers, we teach them to do the same. Creativity is not about winning. Creativity is about creating. But when we ask the question "Why does her daughter have the advantage?" or "Why is his dad making more money than me?" we talk ourselves—and our children—out of creating, and successfully avoid taking our own right action.

Focusing on the competition, to be blunt, is a stalling device for the creative. Because our energy is focused on someone else, usually someone we know, it is especially effective. When we're busy staring at the other person, asking ourselves why things are so unfair, it is hard to turn back to ourselves and ask, "Did my child finish her homework and practice the violin today?"

The truth is, the other person's life has nothing to do with your life. The truth is, the accomplishments of your child's friend do not disempower your child. Your child is empowered by action, and action is always available to take. Anytime we hear ourselves asking, "Why does he have X?" or complaining, "Isn't it unfair?" we must immediately ask ourselves, "What action am I avoiding?"

I have often said that competition lies at the root of much creative blockage. As much as we can model maintaining a healthy focus on ourselves, we help teach our children to avoid the many hours wasted obsessing over what they cannot control (another person's actions) versus what they can control (their own actions).

A woman I know speaks of growing up in the shadow of her talented older brother. Three years his junior, she was always following in his footsteps, but "three years behind," as she put it. She saw herself as less talented than he and struggled not to compare herself with him. Things seemed to come easily to her brother, where her attempts felt belabored, like work. The sibling competition was reinforced in the household as well. "Your brother is very creative," her mother would tell her. Wanting to be like him, she kept following in his footsteps, exacerbating the underlying sibling rivalry. Seeing him study piano and theater, she also studied piano and theater. "He was always supportive of me," she says of her brother. "It wasn't his fault that I saw him as the wunderkind and compared myself to him in everything I did. His success made me second-guess my abilities and creativity. How could I pursue music seriously when I didn't have the same talent as my brother? How could I call myself an actress when I was chorus member number five to my brother's King Arthur?"

Her story is very common, and it is of course human nature to look at those around us and see how we stack up next to them. But we do ourselves a disservice when we decide that another person's path is the model for our own. My friend is, today, an artistic director of a theater. She is a visionary who oversees a large company and her background allows her to often jump into the action herself, helping to light shows, contribute lyrics, adjust costumes when, as she puts it, "someone needs to step in." She appears, today, to be a highly functioning creative professional. "How did you overcome your own insecurities?" I ask her.

"I probably didn't quite overcome them," she says. "But I

learned to rely on myself more and more." She tells me the story of the first summer she went away by herself and stayed with her cousins in Pennsylvania for a couple of weeks, participating in their local community theater. "With my brother nowhere near, and no one in the theater knowing me as 'Sam's sister,' I was free to be myself. I was seen for my own talents and value. I loved the independence and, at age ten, I felt like I had really become an independent woman. I was in rural Pennsylvania, and the theater was near my cousins' house. We were able to walk there on our own and I loved having that kind of autonomy. Growing up in car-dominated suburban Detroit, under the watchful eye of my parents, I felt so free during those summers, personally and creatively."

Focusing on competition, we poison our own well. Focusing on positive effort as opposed to results, we can make great strides. Creating an environment where children are praised for their right actions, we teach them to value the step-by-step nature of accomplishment. Following our example, they learn to take pride in each forward motion of their own, and to appreciate the efforts of their peers as well.

THE NEXT RIGHT THING
An Exercise

There is only ever one action we need to take: the next one. When we are consumed by what someone else is doing, it is time to look at what we are doing. One hundred percent of the time, for us as well as our children, an unhealthy focus on someone else is simply a distracting technique to avoid what we need to be doing ourselves. The good news is that it is very simple to break the spell. The answer to what our next right action is usually well within our awareness.

Fill in the following:

I am distracted by _____, because he/she
is _____.

I suspect that the action I am avoiding in my own life
is _____.

SIBLINGS

With its two pianos, one for study, one for fun, the Cameron house was filled with music. Mother Dorothy played the "Nutcracker Suite" when she was happy and the "Blue Danube Waltz" when she was not. We seven siblings learned quickly how to read her musical cues. My sister, Connie, played music of her own devising, as did my brothers, Jaimie and Christopher. Lorrie preferred classical music, which soothed her when the household became too hectic. The household was seldom without music. Those of us taking music lessons went to the keys to practice. The pianos were almost always "taken" in the Cameron home, and we would have to negotiate with our siblings to get a turn. The rest of the siblings played to the sound of our efforts. Music soaked into our very bones. Both Jaimie and Christopher had a particular knack with the piano. They could improvise by the hour, sometimes making up themes for us girls to dance to.

Once a week we had a piano lesson from Sister Mary Jane.

From her, we learned more formal musical skills, such as reading notes and what to do with our left hands. I was good at playing by ear but not so good at reading music. My sister, Connie, read music fluently but couldn't play much by ear.

Since artists need, above almost all else, support, we must be conscious that we are both receiving this support ourselves and giving it to our children. Unfortunately, many homes allow a natural hierarchy to form, where those children who are excelling receive more attention than those whose efforts are not immediately paying off.

We must all be alert to the tendency to compare our children with one another. Of course, each child is different, and it is natural to note similarities and differences among siblings. Labeling one child "the musical one," however, can knock other siblings out of the running in an area where they may have found joy, and, in time, even excelled.

It's tempting to derail potential sibling competition by simply preventing children from pursuing the same endeavors, but in so doing, we limit our children's freedom of choice. Just because the oldest sibling plays the clarinet does not mean that the clarinet is now "taken" and that the next one must choose something else. By the same token, just because the oldest sibling plays the clarinet does not mean that the next one must also play the clarinet. Encouraging free exploration in our children, we allow them make discoveries and grow as individuals.

My colleague Michael talks about growing up in a family of four. "My siblings and I were all four to five years apart," he says. "We all learned an instrument at some point, and my dad is a sports guy, so we all were required to participate in sports. The ground rules in our family were understood. We all study music.

We all play a sport. We all aim to get good grades. And we all had those things in common. Past that, though, we couldn't be more different."

The four of them, now grown, share a clear set of values, but they have indeed gone in very separate directions. They live in four different parts of the country and are pursuing different things. The oldest teaches at a college in Boston. The second is a nurse in South Carolina. The third stayed in the town where he grew up, teaching second grade at the elementary school he attended. And the fourth is a screenwriter, living in Hollywood.

"They're all different, yes," says their mother. "A couple of them were good at sports, and a couple hated sports. Only one really took to the music, but they all enjoyed it to some degree. I think what I did right was to try to determine their true talents and interests, and encourage them to follow them."

I let her know that her firm insistence on individuality is unusual, and probably accounts for the great success that each of her children now enjoys.

"I don't know if it's unusual," she tells me, "but I knew I had to do it. The worst thing I could do is try to make a kid someone they're not. And just because they're siblings doesn't mean they want the same things. Four people are going to make four lives all their own, eventually. Bottom line, though: everyone has to support each other. That rule is nonnegotiable. No cattiness allowed in my house. If someone wants to try something, don't judge them before they've started.

"Oh, there's fighting," their mother continues. "Still. But there's respect for everyone's voice. We all know that we can trust that."

Making room for—and having respect for—everyone's voice,

we allow impulses to find their way into action and interests to develop into passions. If we set an example of openness, our children will learn to do the same. Older siblings reach out to younger ones, and younger ones inspire the younger still. As we keep a firm grip on instilling an attitude of generosity in the house and a loose grip on how each sibling expresses himself, we raise our children to act on their own behalf while also making way for the ideas and desires of others.

GIFT GIVING

An Exercise

Together with your child, choose someone to whom you will give a gift. The only requirement is that it be something you make yourself. It may be a poem, a song, a drawing. If your child has siblings, assign each of them to give a gift to one other. All will give, and all will receive. Among the Cameron siblings, to this day, we rotate "who has who" and each give our assigned sibling an ornament every Christmas. As a result, we all have full and happy trees adorned with family memories.

PRESSURE

Pressure is put on our children from many angles. In school, teachers may distribute large amounts of homework without any apparent regard for the volumes of work our children are being given in other subjects. Schedules are packed and extracurricular activities abound. Today we have a voice lesson, soccer practice, chores, homework. And we'd better get at least a half an hour of guitar practice in there, since the lesson is coming up on Saturday morning and we missed yesterday. Oh, and by the way, we'd better be excelling in all of these areas. We do want to get into a good college, now, don't we?

In a time where entry into a private-school kindergarten is becoming as competitive as applying to a top college and parents are having their children tutored to get into public school "gifted and talented" programs, we have to protect our children from the endless expectation that more is better, and better is more. When a child has the pressure of being a "great" violinist put on them while they are still learning the basics, they can lose their joy in the process and start to feel that if they aren't already great, they must somehow be a disappointment. When we reward achievement with attention as opposed to rewarding effort and interest, our children start to feel that they deserve our love only when they succeed.

Kristin, a writer, grew up in Manhattan, where her banker parents, with the best of intentions, wanted the best for their only daughter. She was enrolled in top schools from kindergarten through high school. She was exposed to writers and often was able to share her work with authors whom she admired. While she was still in high school, a short story of hers was published in a prominent magazine.

Looking back, she speaks of her experience: "I am grateful. I appreciate that I was lucky. But it was so much, so soon. A lot of the opportunity I had was because of where I lived and who my parents were more than it was because of my own actual talents or interests. It made me grow up so fast. I was a little adult. I wasn't a kid."

Kristin went on to a very selective college, which she describes as "so much easier than high school." Now in her mid-twenties, she is organized and professional. She teaches at a gym while also looking for work as a writer. "My number one problem, though," she tells me, "is that I put so much pressure on myself. Every day, it's like I start at zero. I'm always chasing an impossible, imaginary standard in the distance that I'll never be able to reach."

As Kristin works on her creative recovery now, becoming aware of her right to play and experiment, she reasons that the pressure to succeed, above all else, has made it hard for her to start new endeavors with humility. "I'm only twenty-six," she tells me, "but I feel too old to try something new. I don't want to look bad."

As we raise our young children, we must be alert to the language we use and the messages we pass on. Children are not self-conscious. They are not afraid of "looking bad" as they experiment with new things. Our job is to maintain this environment for as long as possible. And when outside pressures distract them, to remind them that they are valuable and lovable regardless of what they accomplish.

Eric holds a Ph.D. from an Ivy League school. Raised in Philadelphia by first-generation Japanese immigrant parents, he describes the pressures to succeed in his house.

"We all had to excel in school, and we had to excel in other areas, too. We were put in lessons from an early age. For me it was music. For my brother it was golf. Our household was very disciplined and regimented. We were in bed by ten, up by five. We practiced our instrument or sport; we did our homework ahead of schedule. We read books and our parents added all kinds of additional education to our schooling. We were taught, above all, that hard work pays off, and that we had to go to good schools. We both went to Ivy League schools. My brother is a lawyer now, and I became a research scientist. Would I say we are creative, though? I don't know."

Eric now has a daughter. "I am very aware of the academic elitism and of the intellectual snobbery that exists in the world. I hate to say it, but I am not sure I really buy into it—and that comes from someone who spent ten years in postgraduate school!" Adorned with academic privileges and honors himself, Eric rethinks the path he will encourage for his daughter. "Maybe I shouldn't say this," he tells me. "I, of all people, know about advanced degrees. But I actually don't really care if my daughter even goes to college. She's only seven now, and she talks constantly about wanting to be a pastry chef. She's very creative, and I don't want to ever put a lid on that. If she goes to culinary school and opens a bakery like she dreams of, does that make her worse off than me, with my many degrees? I don't think so."

It takes courage for a parent to not pressure their child. Parents often want their children to have what they had or didn't have, they want them to have the "best," they want them to achieve. But if we sit back and observe long enough to see *how* our children are doing—and not just how *well* they are doing—we let them know that their unique voice is heard, and that what they say is worth hearing. Putting pressure on our children to achieve, we are focusing more on the result than on the process. And it is the joyful participation in the process that we must encourage in our households.

BLOWING OFF STEAM
An Exercise

Our children have lots of energy. As much as we may work to relieve the pressure they inevitably gather outside of—and sometimes inside—the home, it behooves us to occasionally plan a family adventure with fun as its only goal. It's best if this adventure is a physical one—visiting the beach, going to a new park or playground, touring a working farm, even going to a theme or water park. Large or small, this adventure should encourage physicality and play. Planning the outing ahead of time as something to look forward to, we can arrange our schedules to make it a priority. And when it is done, it is likely to have rejuvenated—and refocused—us all, thus making us more able to handle, and even thrive in, the inevitable daily pressures we face.

Chapter Eleven

CULTIVATING INDEPENDENCE

~

Teaching our children to practice a healthy autonomy, we teach them to define themselves on their own terms. As we help them to interpret—and sometimes discard—the labels that may be arbitrarily placed on them, we help them to see themselves as they are: an original individual. Teaching them social norms, we also teach them how much to conform. As we strive to be available to them without being *too* available, we help them plant roots as well as grow wings. With a healthy balance of support and independence, we grant them the freedom to be themselves.

IDENTITY VS. LABELS

As we witness and encourage our children's emerging self-definition, we may find ourselves having to draw new boundaries as the erratic forward motion promises change every day. Some boundaries are for our children: "It's okay to sing at the top of your lungs at home in the living room, but if you stand on the table in a restaurant and do the same thing, we'll all be asked to leave." Other boundaries are for ourselves: "Bottom line: I will not say anything negative about my child's creative efforts today. Even if he is making terrible sounds on the trombone, I will only encourage his practice and reward him when the time is up." We also are asked to set boundaries with others: "Do not label my child. Do not compare my children to each other."

As identity forms and our children are allowed choice and measures of independence, we must be conscious of labels. Labels can be uttered carelessly, but stick with people for years. Stephanie studied with the same piano teacher from age six through eighteen. The lesson was a significant event in her week every week for the better part of her upbringing. When Stephanie told the teacher that she was going to college to major in theater, her piano teacher said, "Oh, that's a surprise. I thought it was your brother who always got the leads in the plays."

"I can't believe she said that," she tells me now. "Someone who knew me, too! She was pretty focused on my brother all along—he was her prize student—but it's amazing how carelessly she would just say something like that. And it did affect me, not enough to stop me from doing what I am doing, but certainly enough to make me remember—and repeat—that story several times since."

Creativity is born in generosity and flourishes where there is a sense of safety and self-acceptance. Your child is happiest when feeling a sense of security. As your child's protective parent, you must learn to place your child with safe companions. Toxic influences can poison our children's artistic growth. Not surprisingly, the most toxic influences are those people whose creativity is still blocked. Threatened by the freedom and emerging creativity in our children, they lash out in a jealous, misguided attempt at self-protection.

I ask my students what the greatest block was to their creativity as a child. Hands shoot into the air.

"Being labeled 'non-musical.' Music was my sister's activity."

"My parents telling me to do something productive."

"My father telling me to stop reading and do something useful for once."

"Being laughed at for wanting to dance."

"Having an art teacher yell at me for coloring outside the lines."

"My mom criticizing my drawings."

"My aunt's sarcasm about my poetry."

"My piano teacher telling me to 'never miss a note' in performance. It stopped me in my tracks. I quit piano."

"My mom telling me I was a genius. I thought I had to be perfect. I was embarrassed to ever ask for help."

The list goes on and on. Offhand, thoughtless comments, tossed out and forgotten by the offender, lodge themselves in our psyches and become a block to our creative identities. Labels—

both positive and negative—are dangerous. Telling children they are "lazy" and telling them that they are "brilliant" have similar effects: in both cases, the child is less inclined to do what they might naturally want to do. Called lazy, they feel a sense of shame and "What's the use?" Called brilliant, they are afraid to make mistakes, lest they not live up to their title. The tragic result of both is that in each case, the child learns that creating is dangerous.

Learning that it is dangerous to create, learning that we will be labeled and judged if we create, we respond by not creating. Not creating, we ignore the largest and most precious part of ourselves.

Our culture has a mythology about artists that runs very deep. Teachers, friends, parents may all unconsciously believe that art is a waste of time and that artists are crazy, unstable, alcoholic. The reverse is actually true: blocked artists often act crazy and unstable. Blocked artists waste lots of time. The Great Creator has gifted us with creativity. Every person is creative. Using our creativity brings us closer to God. Encouraging our children's creativity brings our children closer to their own higher power. You must be very careful to safeguard your child's emerging creativity. In protecting them, be gentle but firm, and hang tough. Allow your children the joy of practicing their creativity. Trust that they are on the right track. They are. You need not control their results.

MAKE A COLLAGE
An Exercise

This is one of my favorite exercises, and one for you to do with your children "separately but together." Collect old magazines and give each person a pair of scissors, glue, and a piece of posterboard. As each member of the family chooses images that speak to him or her and arranges them as they like, it is astonishing to note the different messages and beautiful insights each poster contains. This exercise promises to surprise. When you are done, allow each member of the family to "present" his or her collage to the rest.

REBELLION VS. CONFORMITY

We are an ambitious society, and one of the things we are ambitious about is our children. We want them to excel, to shine, to have "the best." We want them to be accepted and we want them to operate successfully in the world. And so, we may find ourselves resisting creative impulses that do not directly serve our children's career goals, or our ideas about what our children's career goals should be. We may resist the things they ask to do that might embarrass us or them—or "make us—or them—look bad." We must be discerning here. There are, of course, accepted norms that we teach our children to conform to in society. And there are other norms that would do well to be challenged a little bit.

It is the paradox of creative recovery—and development—that we must get serious about taking ourselves and our children lightly. We must relearn to play and encourage our children to play. We must protect our children's impulse to expand.

We can find creative ways to encourage "appropriate rebellion"—that is, a sense of play and mischief that can be fun for the whole family. With a little imagination on our part, we can encourage creativity by encouraging a lighthearted nonconformity.

Valerie, mother to an eight- and a twelve-year-old, had tired of her children's constant begging in the cereal aisle at the grocery store. "No, you can't buy cereal if the first ingredient is sugar," she said for the thousandth time. "That would be like having dessert for breakfast." Her children continued to beg, pulling every brightly colored box from the shelf and eagerly reading the list, hoping to find something that they could get past the strict rules of the shopping cart.

"Corn syrup?" Brooke, the older one offered.

"No," Valerie reminded her. "That's sugar."

"But I *want* to eat dessert for breakfast!" her son pleaded. "That would be the best day ever." And suddenly, Valerie had the flash of an idea.

"Well, if you were going to have dessert for breakfast, would you choose cereal?" she asked pointedly. Brooke and Ryan looked at each other.

"Not sure," Brooke said uncertainly.

"You mean if we could have any dessert for breakfast?" Ryan asked.

"Right," Valerie said, and smiled.

"Well, then it would be chocolate cake," the siblings agreed.

"Okay, then," Valerie promised. "Let's go to the baking aisle."

Her children looked at each other, shocked. Were they going to have chocolate cake for breakfast?

"Tomorrow is a special holiday," Valerie continued, pretending to check her calendar. "It's called Backwards Day. That means we start with dessert in the morning, then have dinner. At lunchtime we have lunch, and at dinnertime, we have breakfast." She laughed at how much fun the whole thing seemed, even to her. "So let's plan our menu."

As they raced around the grocery store, deciding on what each meal would be, they anticipated the next day with glee. And as promised, the next morning there was chocolate cake for breakfast. "Now, remember, this only happens once a year," Valerie said. "But it's pretty fun, isn't it?"

From then on, every year, her children looked forward to Backwards Day. This small, creative act of rebellion reminded all of them that they had power in the world, too, that rules weren't set in stone. "Once a year, I don't think it's doing any damage," Valerie says. I am quite sure it is doing the opposite. Playful nonconformity within the guidelines of safety can bring joy and a sense of expansion that it is our spiritual and creative birthright to experience.

A common thread among people who have been raised to become—and remain—freely creative is a sense that their parents enjoyed their playfulness. Without overly praising or harshly discounting their efforts, these parents tended to have a light touch when it came to creative play.

Alexandra remembers going to a summer arts camp as a child, and the day that the director gave each of the participants a parting gift of a necklace with a wooden star pendant on an orange rope. "It takes a brave person to wear orange," he said, handing out the necklaces. Alexandra said it was at this moment her love of orange was spawned. Returning home, she tells the story of deciding that she would take this act of courage even further, proudly sporting every color of the rainbow for her first day of fifth grade: purple shoes, green socks, blue pants, yellow T-shirt peeking out of the neckline of a red polo, and of course, her orange necklace.

"My parents didn't congratulate me on my brilliant outfit when I came downstairs, but they didn't make me go back and change, either," she says. "I guess overall, they pretty much let me do my thing."

Nurturing our children and ourselves, we teach our children to nurture themselves and others. Nurturing themselves and others, they strengthen their connection with the Great Creator. Through this connection, their creativity will unfold. Paths will appear for them. We need not know precisely how. We need to trust that our children are moving in the right direction—and allow them to move out in faith.

BACKWARDS DAY
An Exercise

Taking a cue from Valerie, plan to celebrate a once-a-year festivity: Backwards Day. Allow your children to be involved in the menu. This is a day for exceptions, so don't allow your nutritional goals to overpower this trip to the grocery store. Allow yourself to have fun as well. This will be a day your whole family will remember.

MANAGING AVAILABILITY

It is a constant balancing act to determine how available we should be to our children. There are times when we choose to be un-available, needing to recharge on our own. There are other times when we are committed to work and unable to be at home. And then there are times when we must be cautious not to be *too* avail-able. On a daily basis, our commitments—to ourselves, our work, and our children—must be juggled thoughtfully. It is our job to determine the necessary family schedules. We must meet work and educational needs, appointments and desires. We must also tune in—and react to—emotional and spiritual needs. These help determine the amount of time we have together and the amount of time we have apart.

Often, our impulse is to commit more time to our children than is really feasible—or advisable. We want to be a "good par-ent" 24/7. We believe we should always be "on tap." But this is not realistic. We do our children a disservice if we teach that we will always be available on demand. Better for us to model the real world—a place where we do not always get instant gratifica-tion. When I told my daughter, "Not now, Mommy's writing," I taught her patience and sensitivity. Our children need to learn both of these qualities. When I talk to my daughter on the phone now, she will routinely ask me, "Is this a good time, or are you in the middle of something?" I then give her my boundaries. "I have to leave the house in twenty minutes. We can talk for fifteen." There are times, too, when I am in the midst and cannot talk. My daughter has learned to have faith that I will get back to her as soon as I can. "You need to have time to yourself," my wise friend

Julianna McCarthy taught me. "It's not selfish to take care of yourself. It helps you both." She insisted that I hire a babysitter and that I take the time and care to have a weekly Artist Date, to do something that enchanted or interested me, alone. Julianna insisted that I consciously and regularly "fill the well." As a parent, you draw on your well heavily and must make a conscious effort to replenish it.

When we try to go too long without replenishing our inner well, we run the risk of martyrdom and resentment. Our children can tell when we are available happily and when our availability is a forced march. In tune with ourselves, we take care of ourselves. Taking care of ourselves, we are in tune with our children. Our example of self-care teaches them the same.

When we have to spend extended periods of time at work, we may feel guilty or impatient with a schedule that seems to be beyond our control. But as we accept our schedule and value both our work and home lives, both lives can be richer for it. There is always a happy balance available for us to strike. We can always improve the way we deal with the realities of juggling a work and family life.

David, an entrepreneur, travels frequently for business. "It's part of my reality," he says. His company has three locations, and although his home base is in Miami, he is frequently in New York or L.A. "I have to go," he says. "But my three sons know that whenever I travel, I bring them back a little something. It's really something small—maybe a baseball cap or a book for each of them—but I try to bring a souvenir for each of my kids so that they know I was thinking about them on the road." Although David's work and travel schedule is intense, he keeps in regular contact with his sons, no matter where he is. "I've learned that a little really does go a long way," he says. "Taking ten minutes to really listen to my son's adventures from the day, and tell him I love him, no matter what else is going on, makes us both feel connected. I sometimes wish I could spend all day every day with my kids. But I actually know that it's really okay for all of us the way it is. I just make sure to make an effort every day, no matter what."

David's three sons agree. "Dad knows what we're up to," says Mike, the oldest. "I don't really feel out of touch with him, even though he travels a lot. And he does spend a lot of time with us." When David asks Mike if he'd rather have him around all the time, Mike grins at him. "We have that when we're on vacation. And I think that's enough."

We cannot ignore or completely control the realities of our lives. But the important thing to remember is that we need not be constantly available to our kids. It is the quality of the time, more than the amount of time, that determines our actual relationship with our children.

Too much time, too, can end up backfiring in the end. If our schedule is such that we are indeed with our children most of the time, we have to be alert to not becoming codependent with our child.

Dannie, a stay-at-home mom who also homeschools her daughter, speaks of the opposite issue to David's. "I have to be careful not to be too available to my daughter," she tells me. "We can get enmeshed so easily. Homeschooling is a strong element to add to the already intense mother-daughter relationship. It's the right choice for our family, but it is a balancing act."

Dannie has learned from experience. "When we go too long with 'just the two of us,' we both seem to regress," she tells me. "My daughter needs the checks and balances of a peer group, and since she doesn't have that through school, I have to be very careful to provide it." As Dannie schedules playdates and outside activities for her daughter, she is conscious to put her daughter into situations where other adults are in charge. "It can't just be me, always telling her what to do," Dannie tells me. "She'd resent that very quickly! And I think she'd stop listening."

As we determine right amount of availability for our own well-being and our children's, we juggle realities and desires from every corner. One thing that Dannie learned is that in her own home, it was important to draw limits regarding the parents' bedroom. Although her daughter might have liked to sleep all together, Dannie found this boundary to be especially helpful in a home where enmeshment was a danger. "We let her come into our room at nine a.m. on weekend days to snuggle, but not at other times," she says. "It's good for her to have her own room, her own bed, and a space that's just hers. And the same is good for my husband and me." Sometimes the amount of time we have available to our children is within our control, and sometimes it is not. Keeping an eye on having "enough" time, we must also be alert to not having too much. Giving everyone breathing room, room to "be," we create a family that is at once connected and autonomous.

HOUSE RULES

An Exercise

Creating a list of positive house rules provides both a sense of collaboration and autonomy in the home. Every house is different. The list may contain chores, behaviors, agendas. Allow yourself a little play. Perhaps one of the house rules is that everyone shares a highlight at night.

ROOTS AND WINGS

"The thing about becoming a parent," says Scott, "is that you get to relive your childhood all over again. When my sons experience the thrill of playing in the ocean for the first time, it's like I'm playing in the ocean for the first time, too. I didn't see that coming. It's fun."

Sharing your past with your child can be a thrilling part of parenting. Opening them up to our favorite experiences, we re-experience them ourselves and bond the past and the future. Carrying on our own traditions, we pave the way for our children to carry them on yet again.

"People don't play enough games anymore," says Marcia, a Chicagoland mother of two young boys. "And I'm not talking about video games. I mean games where you have to think. Celebrity, Scattergories, things like that. Parents need to have fun with their kids. And look, going to a sporting event isn't fun for me. Driving them to swimming lessons isn't fun. I mean fun like we used to have when I was growing up. I'm amazed that kids don't know how to play games anymore."

Visiting Marcia's warm and busy home, I watch her navigate the huge amounts of energy coming from her boys and their friends while still staying amazingly focused on talking to me.

"Everyone come over to the table," she calls out. "I'm ordering pizza. And we are going to play a game while we wait for it to arrive."

There is some grumbling, but after a few moments, the boys are assembled at the table, throwing out ideas for pizza toppings and settling roughly in their chairs.

"Okay, okay," Marcia calls out. "I heard you. I have your orders. Now, tell me, do any of you have a clue how to play Scattergories?" Her sons do, but none of their friends do. "Good," Marcia says. "Then you're going to learn."

And so, Marcia lays out the rules and, after a chaotic start, the game is well under way. The boys are entertaining themselves and one another with their answers, connecting with each other in a way that I hadn't seen when they were chasing each other around the house earlier. When the pizza comes, they devour it, but the game doesn't stop.

"See?" Marcia says to them. "More fun than you thought, wasn't it?" Marcia turns to me as the boys scatter. "The thing is, if they haven't tried something, they don't know there's another option. If you never show them that stuff, how do you think they'll learn about it? I happen to believe in games. Car games, games at home—I'll tell you, movies in the car was such a bad idea. I try to set an example of creativity. That's the biggest thing. You want them to read? Read. Play games? Play games with or without them."

Marcia has the right idea, I think, and I tell her this. Her sons are living proof. They are athletes, but they have also both acted in community and school plays. They are learning instruments. They are young boys, and they are moving at the dizzying pace of young boys. But they are being exposed in large and small ways to creative opportunity and to the creativity of the generations that preceded them.

If it is possible to travel to see relatives or to see places where ancestors grew up, it is worth doing. If it is prohibitive to do this, tell stories to your children. Tell them stories of things you remember about growing up. Ask them to tell you a story of their own. If your ancestors are German, go to a German restaurant. Learn to count to ten in German. Open a door—any door—to the rich history of your past, and your child will be enriched.

Sometimes we are able to give roots to our children's dream, but must look to another family member to help provide the wings. When we are able to share our children's development with other members of our family, we are given a rare and precious gift, indeed.

Sarah, a young mom to three-year-old Eva, was never interested in the theater. As a child, her parents valued exposure to as much creativity as possible, taking their children to local productions at the children's theater and area schools. Although Sarah was not tempted to join in the action onstage, she did enjoy spectating, and as much as she might not see herself participating in an activity of the sort, she was entertained.

Sarah's younger brother Toby, however, was an entirely different story. Only three years old when he sat through his first musical, he was immediately entranced by its spectacle. Now a professional theater director, Toby still speaks of his early theatrical memories with the awe of a child.

"I guess it was at the elementary school, the first show I saw," Toby remembers. "But for all I knew it was as mind-blowing as seeing a musical on Broadway for the first time. I couldn't believe my eyes. It felt like real magic to me. In my work, I try to recreate that feeling for my audiences. I always wonder if my former self is sitting in the audience of my shows. I assume he is."

Because Sarah and Toby were raised with the value that creativity in all forms is worth being exposed to, Sarah is committed to giving the same gift to Eva.

"I don't really understand the theater, but Eva seems to enjoy it a lot," Sarah says. "It's not a passion of mine, but I am happy for anything that excites her, really. Her reactions are as fascinating to me as anything happening onstage. I'll always bring her to as much theater as I can. And as soon as she wants to participate, I'll encourage it."

Toby couldn't be more thrilled that his niece seems to be sharing some of his own interests. Visiting her regularly, he brings her movie musicals and CDs. He acts out scenes with her and encourages her to act out her own.

"Eva is really becoming quite the actress," Sarah says, laughing. "I just stay out of the way when she is creating her characters. It's hilarious to me to watch where she goes with these things—constantly making up stories and 'performing' them for me. I'll always be an enthusiastic audience member—now and if ever she decides to do this on a real stage."

Sarah's great gift to Eva is her attention and applause. In giving her this, she does give her roots. Eva has in Toby not only a connection to her extended family but an ally who speaks her language, who offers her gifts a step beyond what she has yet imagined or been exposed to, thus helping her passions take flight. Sarah, in her position from the audience, makes Eva feel safe. Letting her perform her stories in the living room, she gives Eva roots. As an audience, she may seem to perform a non-action, but the gift of attention is perhaps the most important action of all.

As we expose our children to all we can, we give them the possibility of finding not only fun but also connection. Sharing our passions and our histories with our children, we let them know that they are a part of this history and passion. Allowing them to forge connections, we give wings to their dreams.

RETURNING TO GAMES
An Exercise

Play a game. Not a video game. Ideally, you will choose a game you played as a child. Play it with your child today. What memories resurface? How does your child enjoy "playing in your past"?

Chapter Twelve

CULTIVATING FAITH

～

Creativity requires faith, and faith requires that we relinquish control. We are so intricately woven into the fabric of our children's lives that it is easy to feel as though we must play God to our children. We need not. We can consciously bring positive people into their lives, and our own, but our children already have—and will always have—their own unique connection to a higher power. We can forever draw comfort from this. Learning to be of service, our children connect to a larger plan. Through practicing their creativity, our children draw closer to divinity. Each of us contains a divine spark, and that spark can grow into a steady flame. Lit by an inner radiance, our children's lives become lanterns, showing the way for themselves and others.

BELIEVING MIRRORS

Believing Mirrors are people who see the best in us, who mirror us back to ourselves as larger and more expansive than we may feel. They see our potential and respond to our ideas with excitement and faith. We must seek these people out for ourselves, and we must seek these people out for our children. That means not only that we must be a Believing Mirror to our children, but also that we must surround them with other people who will nurture their creativity—not people who try to overly domesticate it "for their own good." Certain of our friendships will inspire our own artistic imagination, while others will deaden it. The same is true of the people we expose our developing children to.

This is not to say that we can control every influence in our lives or in our children's lives. Of course we cannot. Our children are bound to encounter a dud teacher or a mean coach, and it's not a bad thing for them to learn how to deal with people like that. The reality exists that not everyone will play nicely in the world. But ideally, we can work to make sure that the majority of people our children encounter are nurturing and supportive, and we can teach our children to be discerning.

There is a connection between self-nurturing and self-respect. As we nurture and respect our own inner artist, we understand how to nurture and respect our children's inner artists. As we mirror back their largest and greatest qualities, they develop in kind, and grow to fulfill their creative potential.

Creativity is oxygen for our children's souls. Cutting them off from their creativity makes them savage. We ourselves are no different—if we are pushed, day after day, through a schedule that leaves no room for us to stop and notice ourselves, or if we are surrounded by people who squelch us, we begin to react as if we are fighting for our lives. And we are. When we push our children into boxes that do not allow their creativity to evolve, they rebel, react with rage, and act as if they are fighting for their lives. They are.

In speaking to, teaching, and working with many people who have successfully continued a creative practice through childhood and into their adult lives, their answers are very, very similar. Somewhere along the way, a Believing Mirror—or several Believing Mirrors—encouraged them to move forward. Very often, it was a parent. And when it is the parent, the child is in a very good position indeed.

A student in my class is a professional musician. I ask him what allowed him to pursue his dreams, and he answers without hesitation. "My parents. Without a doubt. They have never made me feel foolish or guilty for having an interest in the arts and developing it into a career. They have helped me financially and spiritually in times when I have needed their support more than anything. My dad always tells me how lucky I am to have found my passions and creativity at an early age, that many people are still searching for something to pour themselves into."

How true that rings. I would argue that everyone is searching for something to pour themselves into. We are all meant to create. There are many ways this can manifest, and those who can practice, model, and pass on the act of doing it are the Believing Mirrors we all need.

My self-respect as an artist comes from doing the work. Our

children's self-respect comes from taking creative actions, doing creative work. Consciously championing this, we are telling them, "Your unique perspective matters. I want to hear what you see and think."

Small actions can make a big impact. Peter, an actor, describes his mother's attendance at every single performance he did during elementary school. "I knew she was there to support me," he says. "She never missed a show. Having her in the audience told me that she was happy I was doing this. Knowing she was happy about it, I was allowed to figure out that I was in fact an actor. I was allowed to admit that acting made me happy, too."

Being a Believing Mirror can manifest in other ways as well. When we throw our children onto their own resources creatively, we teach them to look inside themselves. By doing this, we acknowledge that there is, indeed, something inside themselves that is worth looking for. "My stepmom had the most direct impact on my creativity. She would restrict our use of 'lazy' forms of entertainment," says Michele. "We were forced to think of creative ways to entertain ourselves. Because we weren't allowed to watch TV during the day and would rather not do the dishes on a Saturday afternoon, we found other things to do. My introverted brother and I would play 'imaginary friends' while my other brothers played football on the grass island at the end of our street. I didn't have dolls, so I would make 'paper people' out of printer paper. I would spend hours drawing their clothing, little telephones, makeup, and grocery baskets."

Creativity lies in the specific, in the well imagined. It is no coincidence that when people speak of their childhood memories of developing creativity, they speak of specific experiences and events. To be an artist is to recognize and appreciate the particular.

"My passion for comedy comes from my grandfather," Michele continues. "When I was really little, he would sit in front of me and make faces. I remember taking the train to visit him when I was a bit older, and I saw him coming toward me, doing his 'old man' routine. He was there in the distance, limping toward the train, one eye half-closed. When I would do characters for him, at first imitating him and then inventing people of my own, he was my biggest champion. He acted like every face I made was hilarious. He laughed at all of my jokes. His belief that I was funny is what made me believe that I was funny." Today, Michele is an improv comedienne. Her most popular character? The "limping old man."

To kill creative dreams because they are "irresponsible" is to be irresponsible ourselves. The creator made us all creative. Using our creativity, and encouraging others to do the same, is accepting the deal. And accepting the deal is the beginning of true self-acceptance. Accepting others, and reflecting back to them their largest and most expansive self, we become a Believing Mirror. Encouraging our children in small and playful ways, we mirror their potential back to them.

BELIEVING MIRRORS
An Exercise

Take a moment to reflect on your own Believing Mirrors:

A Believing Mirror in my life has been _____.
This person showed me that I _____.

Now examine the landscape of your child's life. Are there Believing Mirrors already there? Are there more you could invite in?

BEING OF SERVICE

Jenna Schwartz was the neighborhood babysitter on a small street in suburban Minneapolis. She had four children of her own and not a lot of money, so she opened her home and offered her services. She would take in practically the whole neighborhood—her motto was "There's always room for one more." Dealing with children often numbering into the double digits, her rule was "Get messy—but clean up." Kids knew that going to Jenna's meant playing crazy games and making lots of mess. Some of the more straitlaced parents on the block questioned Jenna's methods, but they knew their kids loved it.

For her part, Jenna loved her time with the neighborhood children. "The more, the merrier," she caroled. She loved introducing kids to one another, especially when new families would move into the neighborhood. "There's no faster way to meet the neighbors than to come to my house," she'd proudly say. She felt a deep satisfaction as she watched friendships grow among the children, and she said her most satisfying moments were when she was able to make them laugh or help them understand their math homework a little better. "It made me feel so happy," she related. "Like I was making someone's day a little bit better. And that made my day a lot better." Jenna was describing the deep satisfaction that comes from being of service.

My friend Maude says she believes that "teachers and nurses definitely go to heaven." Maude is describing people who dedicate their lives to being of service. With nearly seven decades in a service profession herself, she has seen countless selfless acts of service—many done in silence, with no expectation of reward—that have changed lives for the better.

We can and should be inspired by people whose acts of service enrich our lives. When we are lucky, teachers fill this role for our children. Sharon describes the influence of her son's drama teacher as "life-changing." "Tyler got Peter out of his shell," she says, her eyes immediately filling with tears. "He saw potential for my son to grow, and he wouldn't take no for an answer. He encouraged Peter to try acting, try speech, try comedy. I knew Peter was talented, but I didn't know what he was supposed to do about it. I didn't know how to convince him to perform outside of our living room. Tyler knew how, and I don't know how to thank him for it."

We can look for those great mentors who will influence our children, and we can be of service to our children by encouraging their connection. We need not know how to teach them to dance, but we do need to work it into our schedule to get them to their dance lesson. A father in California tells me that "all" he did was drive his kids to all of their activities. Other than that, he says, he can take no credit for the extremely creative people they became. Well, driving them daily to many lessons over many years was certainly a noble act. His literal and liberal support—of money, time, and energy—made it possible for his kids to develop as they did.

One of his daughters speaks to me now of why she thinks she and her sisters all ended up making their living in the arts. "I think our parents were determined to immerse us in communities and activities where we would be surrounded by creative people. Though my parents are appreciators of the arts, neither of them fully pursued those endeavors in their childhood. My parents' willingness to support me and my sisters through all of those experiences allowed us to be surrounded constantly by other creative people and peers our own age who were interested in the same things."

Those sisters supported each other as well. Siblings can practice the act of generous service by passing down their knowledge to the next one. In the Cameron house, as soon as one of us learned something, we were eager to teach it to our siblings. This form of mentoring is its own reward. Encouraging other people's creative endeavors, our own creative endeavors are fueled. Articulating our support for another's dream, our own dreams are clarified.

HELPING ANOTHER
An Exercise

Today, look for an opportunity where your child can help someone with something. This can be anyone and anything. It may be helping his sibling with his chores, or helping an elderly neighbor in her garden. It may be helping brighten someone's day with a smile or a hug. Let your child know that he may choose his method of help. When it is done, ask him how he enjoyed being of service.

GOD IS IN CHARGE

Creativity takes faith. Faith requires that we relinquish control. But we are the parent—aren't we in charge? Not exactly. We make our best decisions, we listen, and we take action. But underneath all of this is the faith in something larger—the faith that something is guiding our every move, that our instincts are in fact reliable, that God is reliable.

We are not used to thinking that God's will for us and our own inner dreams coincide. We often assume that God's will for us and our will for us are at opposite ends of the table. We believe the message of our culture: Life is hard. Be virtuous. In fact, the opposite is true: Life is beautiful. Live bountifully. We are never alone and our children are never alone. We cannot be everything to our children, yet we can trust that good will come to them. The universe will always support positive creative action. Our truest dreams for ourselves and our children are also God's will for us.

When Domenica was a preteen, she attended public school in Chicago. I had moved her there to place her at a distance from the limelight—her father was becoming more and more famous, and more and more controversial. He made a movie called *The Last Temptation of Christ*. It caused a big enough uproar to reach all the way from New York to Chicago. Domenica's classmates began to tease her unmercifully. At first I didn't take the situation seriously. After all, I reasoned, they were too young to understand. But whether they were young or not, whether they were simply repeating their parents' prejudices, Domenica was the target of their cruelty. She would come home from school in tears. She felt like an outsider and an outcast, but wanted to defend her father's good name. Fortunately, she had an empathetic teacher, Jeff Thornton, who called me in and explained to me that Domenica was indeed being singled out and attacked.

"I do what I can," he said, "but I can only do so much. I'm afraid she sticks out like a sore thumb."

After my talk with Mr. Thornton, I began to explore other options. There were two private schools where Domenica's father's celebrity would blend in with the celebrity of other students' parents. I chose Francis W. Parker School as the best environment. With the support, too, of her father, Domenica transferred to Parker, where her interest in the arts was rewarded with positive attention. She became involved with theater tech, learning to run lighting and sound. She caught the eye of an older boy named Tony. But I still considered her too young to date. Twenty years later, Tony found Domenica again. He asked her to dinner, and a romance followed that led to a happy marriage.

"Mom, he liked me when I had glasses and braces!" Domenica exclaimed.

Creativity—like human life itself—begins in darkness. The process is guided by something larger than we can understand, and we must allow it to guide us.

Mystery is at the heart of creativity. That, and surprise. We must trust the darkness. We must mull—and allow our children time and space to mull—instead of churning ahead like a little engine on a straight-ahead path. The truth is that this is how to raise the best ideas—and the children with the best ideas. Let them grow in the dark and mystery. Offer guidance, but allow them to take their own unique form. We are all born creative. We are all, forever, intended to create.

Today, my beautiful granddaughter, Serafina Rose, reminds me to be open to good, to invite mystery. Holding her tiny hand, I remember: God is the Great Creator.

PRAYER
An Exercise

Write a prayer. It can be short, long, casual, formal. It doesn't matter how you envision or address God. Simply reach out as you would to a good friend. This is for you and you alone.

With thanks to . . .

The Cameron Family

The Lively Family

Tyler Beattie

Sara Carder

Linda Kahn

Joel Fotinos

Susan Raihofer

Index

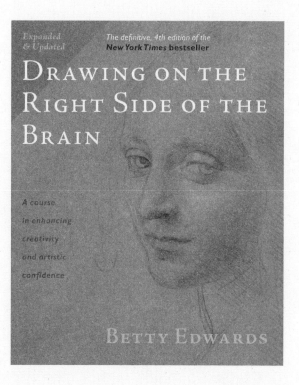

Expanded & Updated

The definitive, 4th edition of the *New York Times* **bestseller**

DRAWING ON THE RIGHT SIDE OF THE BRAIN

A course in enhancing creativity and artistic confidence

BETTY EDWARDS

AN EXPANDED AND UPDATED EDITION OF
THE CLASSIC DRAWING BOOK THAT HAS
SOLD OVER 2 MILLION COPIES.

"Not only a book about drawing, it is a book about living.
This brilliant approach to the teaching of drawing . . . should
not be dismissed as a mere text. It emancipates."
—*Los Angeles Times*

978-1-58542-920-2

$19.95

REVISED AND EXPANDED **1O**TH ANNIVERSARY EDITION

Drawing with Children

A Creative Method for Adult Beginners, Too

MONA BROOKES

author of *Drawing for Older Children & Teens*

This perennial bestseller is the definitive guide for parents
and teachers on how to encourage drawing.

978-0-87477-827-4

$18.95